THE WHOLEMEAL KITCHEN

A harvest of home cooking and baking using the natural goodness of wholemeal flour.

Illustrated on front cover: Profiteroles (page 65).
Illustrated opposite: Leek Pasties (page 112) *and* Little Cheese Squares (page 78).
Illustrated on back cover: English Muffins (page 76) and Pitta Breads (page 75).

By the same author
FAST FOOD — REAL FOOD
MINERALS: WHAT THEY ARE AND WHY WE NEED THEM
THE NEW COOKBOOK
THE RIGHT WAY TO EAT

THE
WHOLEMEAL
KITCHEN
MIRIAM POLUNIN

Illustrated by Ian Jones
Colour photography by John Welburn Associates

THORSONS PUBLISHERS LIMITED
Wellingborough, Northamptonshire

First published 1985

British Library Cataloguing in Publication Data

Polunin, Miriam
The wholemeal kitchen.
1. Cookery   2. Flour as food
I. Title
641.6'311   TX767.W/

ISBN 0-7225-1194-9

Printed and bound in Great Britain

Contents

For Tamzin

Introduction:
Is It Worth
Baking at Home?

If you have given up home baking — or have never started — because you are too busy, or think of flour cookery as unhealthy, fattening stodge, take a fresh look.

This book will provide you with a wide selection of recipes that not only use wholemeal flour, with its extra fibre, vitamins and minerals, but also go much further than most wholemeal recipes to helping you eat in a healthy way.

Today, thoughtful cooks are not interested only in fibre. They also want recipes that use less fat and less sugar. These two ingredients carry a lot of calories for their bulk, even in wholemeal recipes if they simply replace animal fats with vegetable fats or white sugar with brown.

Here is a full range of recipes chosen to provide four key features:

- *More fibre — using wholemeal flour*
  These are not just white flour recipes made with wholemeal flour. They take into account the special properties of wholemeal flour, such as needing extra liquid.

- *Less fat — where possible*
  There's no point in reducing the fat in a recipe if the result tastes worse, or in substituting vegetable fat if the fat used is hardened by a manufacturing process known as hydrogenation. These recipes use the least amount of fat which will still produce a delicious result, and the fats used are those that either have a positive nutritional benefit (such as margarines and oils high in polyunsaturated fatty acids, or 'pufa' for short) or which in small amounts add a worthwhile flavour, such as butter or olive oil.

  Recipes where reducing the fat spoils the result are given in their full, rich state! A little Victoria sponge, croissant or shortcrust pastry, to name the three main items, won't do us any harm provided we team them with a generally low-fat style of eating.

- *Less sugar*
  Brown sugar, however dark and unrefined, has the same number of calories per ounce or gram as white. So the advantage of using brown sugar in place of white is that it contains traces of useful minerals, which contribute to its special flavour. This is too small a difference to make the liberal use of brown sugar healthy. Honey has rather more nutritional advantages, but still not enough to make it healthy if you simply replace your daily sugar consumption with the same weight of honey.

  In this book, honey and sugar are both minimized, but you won't find any lack of sweetness. Fruit purée — simple to make — is often used. It still contains sugars, but they are less concentrated and are accompanied by useful fibre and minerals.

- *Less salt*

  It's surprising how many baking recipes for sweet dishes pop some salt into the ingredients list. Here, salt is omitted where possible. In savoury dishes, as little as possible is used (though individual tastes vary widely). Instead, lemon juice, spring onions, tomatoes, herbs and other seasonings are favoured.

Convenience

You don't have to be devoted to health to find home-baking worthwhile. In spite of the wider variety of bread and cakes available ready-made, the home cook still wins on flavour and cost. What's more, home baking has become much more convenient, in three major ways:

1. Using a freezer makes it possible to batch-bake bread, cakes and savouries. This is particularly advantageous if you slice cakes and bread before freezing, or make small cakes, buns and rolls. This way, individual portions can be defrosted rapidly under the grill or in a toaster or microwave to serve in 2 to 3 minutes as needed.

2. Micronized yeast is yeast in very small particles. This type of yeast is now generally available, and produces a considerable saving of time and effort. It is added dry direct to the flour, cutting out the stage of yeast cookery that many cooks found tricky, the separate mixing of yeast.

3. Adding vitamin C — most easily done with a tub of vitamin C powder (see glossary) — to yeast recipes can literally halve the preparation time. It helps the dough develop so that you need only let it rise once, instead of the traditional twice.

Flavour

Who would deny that home-made bread and other dishes taste better than those bought in shops — unless the shop is the kind of craft bakery where they are almost working on a home-made scale anyway?

It isn't the home cook's skill that is superior, but the use of the best ingredients and being able to take extra care.

While choosing the best ingredients, the home cook can add the extra flavour of wholemeal flour, the only flour that is free from additives as well as containing all the goodness of the wheat grain.

Home cooking opens up a much wider range of wholemeal bread, cakes and biscuits than you'd find even at a wholefood shop. And wholemeal flour can transform food from something that needs excessive amounts of spreads, icing and filling to make it worth eating, to bread and cakes that have real flavour of their own.

Many people who have changed to wholemeal bread say that, where they used to eat their way through umpteen slices of factory-baked white, they find just one or two slices of wholemeal leave them satisfied. It's as though their tastebuds were looking for something in the white bread that just wasn't there.

Wholemeal dishes are not necessarily heavy. For those who need convincing, may I recommend the recipes for Eclairs (page 67) and Kugelhupf (page 24) as proof? On the other hand, many recipes provide a satisfying, something-to-get-your-teeth-into texture that is a great contrast to the all-air, 'high-tech' character of many bought foods.

Cost

With bought bread, cakes, biscuits and ready-made savouries, you really do get what you pay for: the tastiest tend to be much more expensive. Home cooking won't save you money if you compare the cost of your time, as well as of your ingredients, with the price of sticky buns from a mass bakery. But home cooking can give you the kind of quality ingredients in your cakes and biscuits that you'd pay far more for at a craft baker's.

One way in which you can save on bought items is that many are expensively packed, either to prevent damage during their long journey from factory to warehouse to shop, or to look more attractive. A colour-picture carton can cost as much to produce as the item inside!

The more particular you are about the quality of what you eat, the more money you can save by cooking at home compared with the cost of that quality of food in a shop.

Fattening?

The old idea that cakes, biscuits and bread were especially fattening foods was true when most recipes were laden with fats and sugar, and bread heavily spread with butter or margarine or other high-calorie toppings.

On the other hand, nutritionists advise us to eat more carbohydrate, which is certainly not particularly fattening on its own. Why more carbohydrate? Partly because unrefined carbohydrate provides the fibre of which we generally eat too little. Partly because it is very low in fat and, by filling up on pasta, bread, rice, cereals and potatoes, we will have less appetite left for the fatty and sugary foods of which nutritionists want us to eat less.

If you can make cakes and other carbohydrate-based foods in a lower-fat, much-lower-sugar way, you end up with something you can eat and enjoy regularly without consuming excess calories. Using wholemeal flour gives you fibre, as does the dried and fresh fruit used to supply sweetness.

There's also some evidence that people who eat a high-fibre diet find it easier to eat less food. The food is more filling in the stomach, and takes longer to eat, reducing the temptation to gulp it down and have a second helping. One study has suggested that someone eating a high-fibre diet may also absorb fewer of the calories eaten: around 93 per cent, compared with 98 or 99 of every 100 low-fibre calories eaten. This may sound insignificant but, as each of us eats an average of at least 2,000 calories per day, it means a saving of around 80 calories a day, 560 a week or 29,000-plus a year. With around 3,500 calories making up a pound of body weight, that means a high-fibre eater could end up half a stone lighter with no effort at all. Over the years, that can spell all the difference between staying effortlessly trim, and struggling with diets and zips.

Protein

Don't forget that, while flour is mainly carbohydrate, it also provides 16 per cent of its calories in the form of protein. This is exactly the sort of protein level recommended for a balanced diet. So a flour-based dish can make a main course without you worrying about lack of protein. This is good news for all enthusiasts for pasta, pizza, bread pudding and pancakes!

In the past, protein from vegetable sources was often termed 'second class', because it does not provide all the essential protein substances, or else they are present in very different proportions to those present in animal protein foods. Now, such protein grading is considered unnecessary because most of us don't tuck into a single protein food per meal: we mix them. The wheat protein is generally balanced by different kinds of protein in the meal, such as the milk in a sauce or drink, some egg, cheese or beans, or other foods. So a plate of pasta with a vegetable sauce, for instance, will often match up wheat protein with milk in the sauce, or Parmesan cheese on top.

You will find it helpful to read through the Glossary (page 115)
before you start trying the recipes.

Nothing Added

As important as the fact that wholemeal flour has nothing taken away is the fact that it has nothing added.

Other kinds of flour are allowed to contain a variety of improvers, bleaching agents and other additives. Wholemeal plain flour is not.

By making more of your food at home, you can also avoid other additives which are freely used in shop-bought bread and cakes. The goods sold in supermarkets and bakers often have to keep for a considerable time, because they are made in vast batches, often travel long distances and are expected to stay saleable for days, weeks or months on open shelves in warm surroundings. The result is that preservatives are standard. The fact that you buy unwrapped bread or cakes does not mean these additives are absent, only that there is nowhere to label them.

Colours are also widely used in baked goods. This is often to provide the impression that the maker has used the eggs or fruit which would naturally produce that tint — but which have been reduced or omitted for price or preserving reasons. Colours are often accused of being the worst type of additive. Not only may they have ill-effects on some people, which are difficult to trace back to the additive, but they can help the manufacturer deceive the customer about the ingredients in the product they are buying. Although all additives must be labelled on packed goods, an item with an ingredients list including 'blackcurrant flavour, colour' can still suggest to a shopper, both by the words and by its appearance, that it does contain at least some blackcurrants. In fact, it probably contains none. (Incidentally, 'flavour' means just that; a food which genuinely derived its taste mainly from blackcurrants would be described as 'blackcurrant flavoured'.)

It's difficult to argue that colourings are necessary or wanted by customers. What manufacturers do argue is that we, the public, want additives because they keep down the price of processed foods. Additives can make it possible to use cheaper ingredients, with the use of such common items as butter flavour, raspberry flavour, egg replacers and more. Annual sales of additives to UK food manufacturers total over £150 million.

This routine use of additives cannot be laid entirely at the feet of the manufacturers. They do it because the public has been willing to accept this quality of product, and price seems to have top priority on many people's shopping list. In other countries, such as France and Scandinavia, far fewer additives are in use simply because shoppers are more critical of the products they buy.

Now that full ingredient labelling is in force, British consumers seem to be less accepting of additives, with more health doubts being raised, and more resentment of the poor flavour of many processed foods.

A short cut to avoiding most food additives is to 'process' more of your own dishes at home. This is especially appealing if you cook for children. There's increasing evidence that some children who react badly to certain foods also react badly to particular food additives. A yellow-orange colouring called tartrazine (or E102) is now a 'dirty word' to many parents. Yet it happens to be one of the most commonly used colourings in bought biscuits and cakes.

One additive you can't easily avoid by cooking at home is the preservative sulphur dioxide. It is present on all pale dried fruit — it helps keep it pale. This includes dried apricots (unless you buy either Hunza or 'unsulphured' darker apricots), sultanas, apple rings, dried pears, dried peaches, and dried nectarines.

It has been suggested that sulphur dioxide can irritate the digestive canal, perhaps because it destroys some of the B vitamins in food which are involved in digestion. Avoid long-stored foods treated with sulphur dioxide: they can develop a most unpleasant flavour, and may be more irritant. Boiling dried fruit in water for 1 or 2 minutes, then draining and starting again, should reduce the amount of sulphur to some extent.

When buying dried fruit, look at the label and avoid types treated with white mineral oil, also known as liquid paraffin. Apart from the disagreeable prospect of downing this formerly popular laxative, you may well want to avoid white mineral oil because it might hinder your body from absorbing some of the fat-soluble vitamins (A, D and E) from your food. Health and wholefood stores sell unoiled fruit, and some packers use vegetable oil as a lubricant instead.

1.
Why wholemeal?

What does wholemeal flour do for you that white flour doesn't? The chart on page 14 shows the nutritional gap between wholemeal and white flour, which goes far beyond the now-famous fibre. While we tend to be aware of the protein and main vitamins in food, lesser-known vitamins and minerals are just as important to good health.

If bread and other flour-based foods formed only a small amount of our meals, their food value would be less important. But now, when millions of us are keen to eat more fibre-rich foods and fewer high-fat animal foods, the food value of flour becomes far more significant.

Less than three-quarters of the wheat grain is used in white flour. And the 28 to 30 per cent of the wheat grain which is removed is the part richest in food value. While the endosperm — the main element in white flour — is like a larder of starch for the growing wheat seed, the wheat sprout or germ itself, and the outer, or bran, layers are far richer in protein, vitamins, minerals and essential fatty acids, as well as in fibre.

Wheat germ, for instance, contains over 25 per cent protein, — higher than most kinds of meat — as well as generous amounts of the B vitamin group and of vitamin E. Bran also provides protein, B vitamins and some minerals as well as roughage.

As well as the minerals on the chart, other 'trace elements' are largely lost from white bread during refining from wholemeal. Trace elements are also vital to health. Those reduced by refining flour include chromium, selenium, cobalt and molybdenum.

Fibre

Fibre or roughage used to be completely ignored as an element in human health, but in recent years it has become one of the biggest talking points in the medical world.

It has been realized that, although fibre contributes few calories, it provides a kind of 'padding' which the digestive system requires. At first, the bulk provided by fibre as it passed through the body, absorbing water, was thought to be useful only in preventing constipation. Now it's thought that fibre has much more complex effects on the digestive system. In the stomach, it absorbs fluid and so makes food more filling. It can slow down the absorption of food, so that the blood sugar level rises more gradually after eating. This sounds bad, but it means that energy is delivered more gently to the body. It's an effect that is particularly useful for those whose bodies deal poorly with a sudden mass of food, especially sugary foods — notably diabetics, but many other people as well.

In the lower digestive system, however, fibre tends to speed up the passage of food through

The Nutritional Content of Different Breads

| Bread | Calories* | Fibre* | Magnesium mg | Calcium mg | Iron mg | Zinc mg | Potassium mg | per 100g (3½ oz) | | | | | | |
								Vitamin B1 mg	Vitamin B2 mg	Vitamin B3 mg	Vitamin B6 mg	Pantothenic acid mg	Biotin mcg*	Vitamin E mg
Wholemeal	61	2.4	93	23	2.5	2.0	220	0.26	0.08	5.6	0.14	0.6	6	0.2
Brown	63	1.4	75	100*	2.5*	1.6	210	0.24	0.06	4.7	0.08	0.3	3	trace
Wheatgerm	65	1.3	60	150*	4.5*	—	210	0.52	0.1	5.9	0.09	0.3	2	trace
White	66	0.8	26	100*	1.7*	0.8	100	0.18*	0.03	3.00	0.04	0.3	1	trace

*per oz (28g)   *grams per oz (28g)   *millers add extra calcium   *includes added iron   *includes extra added by miller   *includes extra added by miller   *micrograms

the yards of digestive tract. This is thought to be because it gives the muscle rings which surround the digestive tubing, squeezing food along by their contractions, a bigger bulk to grip on so they work better. In the bowel, the larger bulk of waste products sets off the nerve signal 'empty me, please' more effectively.

The speedier movement of food through the intestine is considered another reason why fibre is important for health. It prevents the muscle rings struggling to grip small, hard wastes, by providing more bulk. The effort of the muscles to grip is thought to increase pressure in the tube, which can lead to 'blow-outs' in the walls between muscle rings. These 'diverticula' are very common in westerners. They may give no trouble but, if food wastes get stuck in them, infection and inflammation can result, not to mention much pain, and surgery may be necessary. Pressure in the lower intestine, resulting from lack of fibre, is also blamed for some other digestive problems, such as some cramping in mucous colitis. Pressure caused by the effort of pushing out small hard wastes is now thought to be a major cause of piles or haemorrhoids, and to contribute to varicose veins too.

Finally, some doctors — still controversially — link lack of fibre in western food with the rise of cancer of the bowel, now the second most common fatal cancer in the United Kingdom. The theory is that low-fibre food lingers longer in the bowel, and that harmful elements which the body would otherwise dispose of quickly, or which develop during the longer bowel stay, may start trouble when in contact with the delicate bowel wall.

Whole wheat is far from the only source of fibre, but it is a main one in a wheat-eating country. It is far healthier to get your extra fibre from eating more wholemeal foods rather than sprinkling bran on food. This is partly because wheat bran contains a substance which can combine with calcium, iron or zinc, to form a compound from which the body cannot extract these useful minerals. But when bran is incorporated into bread, the fermentation and cooking process result in much of this substance — phytic acid — being broken down, so that fewer minerals are 'locked up'. The other reason for preferring high fibre foods to bran is that by using unrefined foods — cereals, beans and peas — you get the benefit of their vitamins and minerals as well as of their fibre.

Wholemeal food is also a far tastier way of eating fibre! The 'bran with everything' craze led to many people taking so much that, when it absorbed fluid inside them, they felt blown out and flatulent. There's no harm in adding a little bran to food, especially if you are in the habit of taking laxatives and would like to prevent constipation by natural means. But only add a few teaspoonsful, and at the same time eat more fibre *in* foods, and take more exercise to tackle your constipation most effectively.

For ideas on building extra fibre into food, see Chapter 12 (page 110).

2.
How to Choose the Right Flour

Ask most people about flour and they'll tell you that it's plain or self-raising, brown or white. This is only part of the story. Here are three main distinctions.:

- *'Strong' or 'weak'* are adjectives describing the amount of gluten in different varieties of wheat, and thus in different flours.

  'Strong' flour contains a lot of the protein that forms gluten when mixed with water. When made into a dough, this flour forms elastic strands which will stretch a long way without breaking: they are literally 'strong'. When yeast or baking powder in a recipe produces gas, the strands of dough stretch, and the bread or cake rises as the gas is captured in the strong elastic dough. 'Strong' flour is preferred for bread, pasta, strudels, croissants and some other recipes where you want to hold a lot of air, or you need a dough which can be stretched very thin without breaking.

  A 'weak' flour is more suitable for cakes and biscuits, where you don't want these qualities. 'Weak' flours are often called 'soft'. Strong flour is sometimes called 'hard', and it can produce a tough effect if used in cakes. The nature of the flour depends partly on the variety of wheat, and partly on the climate where it is grown.

  Most of the flours you can buy are a combination of 'strong' flours imported from Canada or North America, and 'soft' British-grown ones. In the last decade, British farmers have been turning to varieties of wheat that are 'stronger', because these command a higher price. It's important to remember that 'weak' and 'soft' don't mean poor quality, just different.

  Recipes here show where strong flour is an advantage.

- *100, 85, 81 per cent or 'brown'* are descriptions on flour labels of how much of the wheat grain is used in the flour. 100 per cent clearly means wholemeal, which is legally the same as wholewheat, 'the whole of the product of cleaned wheat'.

  85 per cent flour, usually produced from a roller mill, has had 15 per cent of the wheat held back, almost all bran.

  81 per cent flour was developed because of the law on fortifying white flour with two of the vitamins and two of the minerals reduced by refining it from whole wheat.

  The law is that the levels of vitamins B_1, B_3, iron and calcium must be restored to the levels naturally occurring in 80 per cent flour (i.e., flour where 80 per cent of the

Opposite: Irish Soda Bread (page 27) *and* Cinnamon Orange Scones (page 21).

wheat grain is retained). In deference to those people who wanted flour with nothing added, millers produced 81 per cent flour. As well as containing the legal minimum of the four nutrients mentioned above, it will contain slightly more of the other minerals and vitamins affected by the usual refining, which is to around 72 per cent of the wheat.

Its other major attraction is that it is unbleached. The maturing/bleaching agent used in most white flour has been under health suspicion for many years.

With the increasing interest in fibre, the use of 81 per cent flour has declined. It's mainly used as a starting point for those turning to more natural foods. Another reason why it is less popular is that the cook can produce something very similar when a paler flour is wanted, by sieving wholemeal flour and keeping aside bran left in the sieve. This is basically how 81 per cent flour is produced anyway. The sieving method may not remove exactly 19 per cent of the flour, but will certainly produce a less branny flour which, as bran somewhat impedes rising, will produce more 'lift' in scones and sponges. The retained bran can still be used elsewhere in cooking, so the fibre intake stays up. The cook has the convenience of only having to keep one type of flour.

Brown Flour legally covers all flour which has a minimum of 0.6 per cent crude fibre, but which isn't wholemeal/wholewheat. So the term can appear on flour which is rather pale (except it may be 'browned up' with caramel) or on flour which is almost wholemeal. Granary flour is a trademarked product, which has a higher-than-average (though lower than wholemeal) fibre content. Hovis has less fibre, although there are now high-fibre wholemeal versions under this brand.

Wholemeal flour remains the most useful flour for the cook. It can be sieved to produce a paler flour where wanted, but is suitable in its natural state for many purposes as well as for bread. You can use all-purpose versions, or keep this plus a strong variety for some recipes.

- *Stoneground or roller-milled.* Most wholemeal flours used to be stoneground. This method, which dates back as far as 4000BC (the British Museum has stones from this era), crushes the wheat grain in one single operation between two large grooved stones, the top one revolving to give the crushing movement. Stonegrinding is preferred by many people to the alternative method brought into general use about 100 years ago, roller-milling. The preference is partly nostalgia, partly for what enthusiasts say is its better flavour, and partly because the miller can't cheat. The flour automatically contains all the grain, including the germ and bran. In roller-milling, the grain is fed through a series of steel rollers and sieves. The rollers have raised surfaces designed to break down the wheat grain neatly, removing the bran layers and wheat germ in sequence. The miller ends up with separate piles of different parts of the grain. To make wholemeal flour, he adds them back together again, although he could keep out some parts to produce 'brown' flour. This method is increasingly used to satisfy the huge demand for wholemeal flour over recent years. There is no reason to think that the big brands of wholemeal flour or bread are not really wholemeal. But many people still prefer the stoneground versions.

Nutritionally, there may be an advantage in stone-grinding because the flour may not get so hot as in the faster roller-milling. Heat is damaging to B vitamins. The flour certainly

Opposite: Alternative Sponge Cake (page 23) *and* Victoria Wholemeal Sponge Cake (page 22).

gets warm in stone-grinding, and the wheat germ oil gets evenly spread through it. This may account for people saying it has a different flavour or behaves differently in cooking. Try both and decide for yourself. But don't think that 'stoneground' means the only wholemeal.

You can buy wholemeal flour in *plain or self-raising versions*. Which to buy will depend largely on what you intend to cook with it. As many recipes, including bread, crêpes, all yeast cakes and buns, pastry and more, require plain flour, it's often more convenient to add your own baking powder to suit the recipe.

Raising agents are a mixture of acid and alkaline chemicals which react when heated to produce carbon dioxide gas. As this gas is formed, it makes bubbles in the mixture forcing it to rise. The reaction begins when the raising agents meet liquid, so recipes using baking powder should be baked as soon as possible once liquid has been added.

Baking powder has two nutritional disadvantages. First, it destroys some of the B vitamins in the food, especially thiamine (B_1). Around a third of the B_1 will be lost, compared to 20 per cent loss in any baked food just from heat. Second, bicarbonate of soda is high in sodium. People on low-sodium diets can either stick to yeast-raised recipes, buy low sodium *Salfree* baking powder from a health food store or chemist, or ask a pharmacist to make up this mixture:

28 grams starch
7.5 grams tartaric acid
39.8 grams potassium bicarbonate
56.1 grams potassium bitartrate

Use 1 heaped teaspoon per 8 oz /225g flour.*

Yeast recipes are stressed throughout this book because of these nutritional advantages. A third advantage is that cakes and buns made with yeast require far less sugar and fat. This is because they are needed only as flavourings, or moisteners, while in other recipes, they are often essential for the whole texture and success of the recipe. However, traditional recipes which include baking powder are also provided.

Non-Wheat Flours

In this country, when we think of flour, we think of wheat flour. But other flours are growing in popularity because of interest in foreign cooking and for gluten-free diets.

While wheat starch, without the wheat protein that contains gluten, is available, it is highly refined, low in fibre and poor in flavour. Flours from foods which are naturally gluten-free are preferable. These are: brown rice flour, buckwheat flour, potato flour, maize flour and soya flour.

Here are some ideas for enjoying non-wheat flours:

Rye flour	Bread: mix ⅓ — ½ rye flour (more makes grey, sticky dough) with ⅔ — ½ wheat. Look out for 100 per cent whole rye flour.
Buckwheat flour:	Pancakes (traditional American thick ones; or Breton crêpes; or Russian blini with yeast). Gluten-free recipes.

* Recipe taken with permission from *The Salt-Free Diet Book* by Dr Graham MacGregor (Martin Dunitz, London).

Barley flour:	Bread: use same proportions as for rye flour.
Potato flour:	Pancakes: traditional in Northern Europe. Also some continental cakes. Gluten-free recipes.
Rice flour:	Oriental recipes; gluten-free bread and other gluten-free recipes.
Maize flour:	Tortillas and American 'johnny cake' recipes. Gluten-free.
Soya flour:	Adds protein, vitamins and flavour, but does not behave like grain flours, so used in small amounts with other flours. Popular with vegetarian cooks. Gluten-free.

All these flours, except soya, can also be used for thickening.

Freezing What You Make

Bread, rolls and cakes can all be frozen for at least two months and most cakes can be frozen for four.

The best results are obtained by freezing food when it is very fresh, but completely cool. Freeze sponge and other filled or frosted cakes before filling or icing.

Biscuits:	can be frozen but keep well in airtight tin. Spare dough can be frozen and thawed to bake into biscuits as wanted.
Bread:	freezes well, as do rolls. When thawed, they stale quicker than the fresh versions, so thaw only what you need. Thaw in wrappings for 2 — 3 hours, or wrap loaf in foil and thaw at 400°F/200°C (Gas Mark 6) for about 30 minutes. Rolls or scones can be placed in same temperature oven and re-heated in 15 minutes. Slices of bread can be toasted from frozen.
Cakes:	thaw at room temperature in freezer wrappings. They will stale quicker than fresh so use immediately, or freeze cakes in slices or segments so you only thaw what you need.
Pancakes:	crêpes and drop scones can both be re-heated in a hot skillet brushed with oil in about 25 seconds each side. They should be packed with layers of polythene between to separate them when frozen.
Pasta:	fresh pasta can be frozen, cut into shapes, and plunged straight into boiling water for about 5 minutes. Cooked pasta dishes can be cooked, covered for about 40 minutes, then uncovered for a further 10 to brown, at around 400°F/200°C (Gas Mark 6).
Pastry:	can be frozen as dough or baked. The former produces a very quick source of pastry provided you remember to put out to thaw, or have a microwave cooker. Baked pastry shells or tartlets should be frozen unfilled. Heat oven to 350°F/180°C (Gas Mark 4) and re-heat, filled, for 15 minutes or until filling is ready.
Sandwiches:	omit salad or mayonnaise fillings. Stack a number of rounds in one freezer pack, each in a separate bag if you wish to remove one pack at a time. A sandwich removed from freezer to lunchbox at around 8 a.m. will be ready to eat by 12.30 p.m.
Steamed puddings:	cook puddings in freezer-proof basins or other shapes. When cool, bag the basin. To serve, thaw for about 2 hours, then steam for about 45 minutes, or as directed for Christmas pudding.

3.
Baking at Home
is Child's Play

Before the arrival of mass-produced buns and cakes, home cooks were as familiar with baking as they are now with boiling an egg. The air of mystery that many younger women feel surrounding baking is an illusion. You don't need a lot of time or skill to bake well, and the habit of home-baking not only produces delicious and popular results, but also gives the baker a lot of satisfaction. It's only recently, as people become concerned about the quality — both in terms of health and flavour — of the food they eat that a revival of interest in home baking is obvious.

Baking is not difficult. Even if your cooking skill stops at serving up beans on toast, you can turn out professional (but tastier) results.

This chapter is for those who want to start baking with wholemeal flour: it contains only basic recipes that will work easily, and encourage you to move on to more.

Those readers who are old hands at baking may think that this chapter does not apply to them, but if you're new to wholemeal flour, have a go. Apart from anything else, they're easy and useful additions to your range: really child's play!

Earl Grey Tea Bread

Use dried apricots for about a third of your dried druit for a particularly delicious flavour to this delightfully simple fruit loaf.

Imperial (Metric)

9 oz (250g) mixed dried fruit, washed and chopped if using apricots or peaches
7 fl oz (200ml) strong Earl Grey tea or favourite variety, strained
2 tablespoons clear honey
1 large egg, beaten
9 oz (250g) wholemeal flour
2 teaspoons baking powder
1 oz (25g) high pufa margarine (see Glossary)

Topping:

¾ oz (20g) walnuts, chopped
1 tablespoon clear honey

1. Place dried fruit, tea and honey in bowl to soak overnight.
2. Next day, set oven to 350°F/180°C (Gas Mark 4).
3. Add to dried fruit mixture the egg, flour, baking powder and fat. If necessary, add a little water to make a dropping consistency.
4. Grease a 7-inch (18cm) cake tin or large loaf tin. Transfer mixture.
5. Bake for 45-55 minutes, until firm. Remove from oven, brush cake top with the honey, then press in the nuts. Bake for a further 10 minutes before cooling on rack.

Scones

Makes about 8-9, 2 inch (5cm) square scones.

A handy recipe for hungry children, unexpected guests and when you run out of bread, this takes 15 minutes start to finish. Square scones are quicker to cut, and avoid re-rolling dough scraps.

Imperial (Metric)

8 oz (225g) plain wholemeal flour
½ teaspoon bicarbonate of soda
1 teaspoon cream of tartar
Pinch of sea salt (optional)
2 oz (55g) high pufa margarine
¼ pint (140ml) skim milk

1. Set oven to its highest temperature.
2. Sift flour with soda, tartar and salt if using, retaining bran left in sieve on one side.
3. Rub fat into flour, then add enough milk to make a very wettish, soft dough.
4. Use retained bran to 'flour' worktop, then pat out mixture about ¾-inch (2cm) thick.
5. Cut desired shapes and place on greased baking sheet.
6. Bake for 10-12 minutes, until just firm.

Variations:
Cheese Scones: Just before adding milk, add 3 oz (85g) mature or reduced fat Cheddar cheese, grated, to the mixture with 1 teaspoon dry mustard and ½ teaspoon dried sage or thyme (crumbled) if wished. For extra flavour sprinkle scones lightly with Parmesan cheese before baking.
Cinnamon Orange Scones (*Illustrated opposite page 16*): Before adding milk, add 2 teaspoons finely grated orange rind, 1½ teaspoons ground cinnamon and 1½ oz (45g) washed currants or sultanas to the mixture. Liquidize the milk with 2 teaspoons honey and 1½ oz (45g) more washed dried fruit, plus half the flesh of the orange.

Victoria Wholemeal Sponge Cake

Illustrated opposite page 17.

There's no way of making a low-sugar sponge cake, although you can reduce the fat if you don't mind the cake staling within 24 hours. This is the traditional method, with a little water added because wholemeal flour absorbs more liquid.

Imperial (Metric)

6 oz (170g) Demerara sugar
6 oz (170g) high pufa margarine
3 eggs, beaten
6 oz (170g) plain wholemeal flour
2 teaspoons baking powder
1-2 tablespoons cold water

1. Grease and line the bases of two 7-inch (18cm) sandwich tins. Set oven to 375°F/190°C (Gas Mark 5).
2. Cream sugar and fat until pale and fluffy. Beat in eggs a little at a time, beating thoroughly after each addition.
3. Sift flour and baking powder, keeping back any bran left in the sieve. Use some of this to 'flour' the greased tins, and keep remainder for another recipe or mix with the filling.
4. Using a large metal spoon, lightly fold half the flour into the creamed mixture, then the remainder. Add water to make a soft consistency.
5. Divide mixture between the tins and use the tablespoon to level. Now make a slight depression in each centre to avoid peaks.
6. Bake for about 20 minutes until cakes just shrink from tin sides. Leave a minute or two in tins before turning on to rack to cool.

Fillings:

See Glazes and Fillings in the Glossary.

Variation:
To make a Swiss-roll, bake mixture in Swiss-roll tin. Turn out on to a dampened wrung-out teatowel, topped with a piece of greaseproof paper, so cake is on paper. Spread with jam or chosen filling. Make a cut half way through the depth of the cake, running across narrower side, about 1 inch (2.5cm) from end. Turn this end over firmly, then use the greaseproof paper under cake to roll the cake up away from you. Wrap firmly in the paper to set for 5 minutes. Unwrap, cool on wire rack with 'seam' downwards. Dredge if liked with a little sugar which has been powdered in a coffee mill or using a rolling pin.

Victoria Sponge Cake

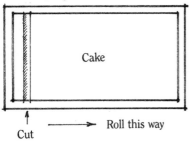

Cake

Cut

Roll this way

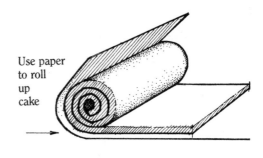

Use paper
to roll
up
cake

Alternative Sponge Cake

Illustrated opposite page 17.

A cake for those who want something sponge-like, and who also want to have their cake —
and eat it with less sugar and less fat. Here, you 'save' fat on the proportion of fat to flour,
the skim milk and by using egg whites only.

Imperial (Metric)

2¼ oz (70g) high pufa margarine
6 tablespoons (90ml) clear honey
7½ fl oz (215ml) skim milk
A few drops natural vanilla essence
10½ oz (300g) plain wholemeal flour
3 teaspoons baking powder
3 eggs whites, stiffly beaten

1. Set oven to 375°F/190°C (Gas Mark 5).
2. Heat fat and honey gently until just melted. Remove from heat and add the milk and
   vanilla.
3. Sift the flour and baking powder, retaining bran left in the sieve.
4. Thoroughly grease two 7-inch (18cm) sandwich tins and 'flour' with some of the
   retained bran. Keep any extra bran for another recipe, or add to the filling.
5. Add milk mixture to flour, then fold in egg whites carefully.
6. Transfer mixture to cake tins, make small depression in centre of each to discourage
   peaks forming.
7. Bake for 20 minutes, or until cakes just shrink from tin sides. Leave in tins for a
   minute or two before cooling on a rack.

Fillings:

See Glazes and Fillings in the Glossary.

Kugelhupf

An excellent introduction to yeast cakes, this makes a very light cake that will impress those who expect wholemeal baking to be solid. Do use strong flour.

Imperial (Metric)

12 oz (350g) strong plain wholemeal flour
1 rounded teaspoon micronized yeast
Generous pinch of vitamin C powder
7 fl oz (200ml) skim milk, warmed to 110°F (43°C)
1 tablespoon honey
2 eggs, beaten
3 oz (85g) high pufa margarine (see Glossary) or softened butter, or a mixture
3 oz (85g) currants, washed
3 oz (85g) sultanas, washed
3 oz (85g) raisins, washed
About 24 blanched almond halves, roughly chopped

1. Sieve flour, setting aside any bran left in sieve.
2. Mix all ingredients except almonds, stirring 50 times to make a very thick batter.
3. Grease mould. Sprinkle with the almonds, then with the retained bran. (Use any extra bran for another recipe.)
4. Spoon mixture into tin, cover with polythene. Leave in a warm place until dough has doubled in size. This may take 1-1½ hours because rich doughs rise slower.
5. Heat oven to its highest temperature. Bake cake for 10 minutes, then reduce heat to 375°F/190°C (Gas Mark 5) for further 40 minutes or until cake is shrinking from sides of pan.
6. Leave in tin for a few minutes before cooling on a wire rack.

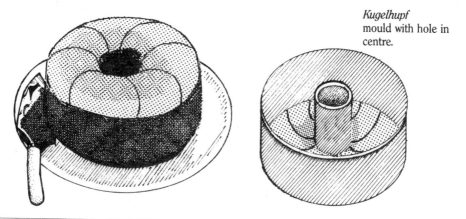

Kugelhupf mould with hole in centre.

Wholemeal Shortcrust Pastry

To line an 8-inch (20cm) flan case or make 12 tartlet bases.

Wholemeal pastry is more crumbly, but this is no problem if you remember two simple rules: add a very little more water, as wholemeal flour absorbs more, and roll out on foil or polythene so you can lift pastry easily.

Imperial (Metric)

8 oz (225g) plain wholemeal flour
4 oz (115g) high pufa margarine
Very cold water to mix

1. Rub fat into flour, using a fork or fingers.
2. Add very cold water very cautiously, just until mixture will bind together.
3. Do not knead. Roll out on a sheet of polythene or foil to desired shape. This helps prevent cracking, and makes it easy to line a baking tin by inverting pastry and backing sheet over tin, then peeling off sheet of polythene or foil. (Avoid using a printed polythene carrier bag, as the ink may come off.)

Note:
For more convenient pastry making, when making a batch, double the size. After rubbing in, place half the mixture in sealed container in refrigerator. When you need pastry, you need only add water and roll out. This is as convenient as bought pastry, and much cheaper.

Spare pastry can be flavoured by adding some grated mature Cheddar cheese, a little dry mustard and some pepper, and cut into biscuits to bake for 15-20 minutes at 375°F/190°C (Gas Mark 5).

You can't reduce the fat in shortcrust pastry by any significant amount without spoiling the result. The most you can change the ratio is to use about 60 grams of flour to each 25 grams of fat.

Yeast Pastry

Makes enough for 2 small or 1 very large 'strudel' or pie.

A traditional Eastern European pastry that avoids the high level of fat involved even in wholemeal shortcrust pastry. Delightfully easy to work with.

Imperial (Metric)

7 oz (200g) plain wholemeal flour
1 oz (25g) high pufa margarine, softened butter or vegetable oil
1 teaspoon micronized yeast
Pinch of sea salt
1 egg, beaten
About ¼ pint (140ml) warm water, to mix
Large pinch of vitamin C powder

1. Mix all the ingredients, adjusting amount of water to make a soft dough, and reserving a little egg for glazing finished pastry.
2. Turn on to a floured worktop and knead for 5-8 minutes.
3. Cover with upturned mixing bowl or sheet of polythene until wanted. If you want to keep the pastry for several hours before using, place in tightly covered container in the refrigerator. Dough will rise, but won't spoil for around 24 hours. To use, pull into a ball but do not re-knead.
4. Roll out thinly (it will thicken a little on baking) to desired shape. Fill or top as desired, and brush with beaten egg. Bake for about 20 minutes at 425°F/220°C (Gas Mark 7). If using a filling such as raw fish, bake for 30 minutes at 400°F/200°C (Gas Mark 6), reducing heat to 350°F/180°C (Gas Mark 4) if pie starts browning too much. You can also protect the pie top from over-browning by covering with foil halfway through cooking time.
    If using a filling that takes longer cooking, pre-cook at least partially before combining with the pastry.

Note:
This pastry is most suitable for filling (e.g. pasties) or wrapping (e.g. apple dumplings). Spare pieces can be frozen until wanted.

Irish Soda Bread

Makes 1 large farl. Illustrated opposite page 16.

Simple and popular whenever you want fresh bread.

Imperial (Metric)

1 lb (450g) plain wholemeal flour
Large pinch of sea salt
1 teaspoon bicarbonate of soda
2 teaspoons cream of tartar
1 oz (25g) high pufa margarine
Generous ½ pint (285ml) skim milk or buttermilk
1 teaspoon honey (optional)

1. Heat oven to maximum temperature.
2. Sift flour with salt, soda and cream of tartar, adding back any bran left in sieve.
3. Fork in the margarine. If using honey, whisk into the milk with a fork. Add milk to mixture to make a *very* moist dough. If necessary add a little water to achieve this consistency.
4. Tip dough on to a well-greased baking sheet and pat into a flat round about 9 inches (23cm) across.
5. Brush with milk, make 2 deep cuts across dough. Bake for 10 minutes, then for further 20-25 minutes at 400°F/200°C (Gas Mark 6). Cool on wire rack.

Variation:
For **Cheese Soda Bread**, add 1 teaspoon dry mustard to the flour when sifting, and 3 oz (85g) mature Cheddar cheese, grated, with ½ teaspoon crumbled dried sage before adding milk. Sprinkle farl with 1 oz (85g) more Cheddar cheese or grated Parmesan before baking.

4.
Main Courses

The protein value of wholemeal flour means that you can base a main course on it without worrying about lack of protein, even for growing teenagers or heavy workers.

Flour-based main courses have four important advantages over the meat-and-two-veg pattern:

1. You get the protein with much less fat than most meats, cheese or eggs provide. You don't have to become vegetarian to enjoy some meatless main courses. On the other hand, it's very difficult to have a healthily low level of fat in your meals if every main course includes meat or dairy foods.

2. You get fibre built in when you use wholemeal flour.

3. Your housekeeping bills go down if you base more meals on popular dishes such as pizza, crumbles or pasta, with or without small amounts of meat or fish, versus the cost of meaty main meals.

4. You don't have to add potatoes, rice or other 'fillers'. These dishes usually make a meal in themselves; all you have to add is salad or lightly-cooked fresh vegetables. This makes these meals highly convenient.

Cheese Soufflé

Serves 3-4

Never fails — provided you get your eaters to table before it comes from the oven so it doesn't have time to sink. Good with rice and broccoli.

Imperial (Metric)

1 oz (25g) high pufa margarine or butter
2 tablespoons plain wholemeal flour
¼ pint (140ml) skim milk
3 oz (85g) mature Cheddar cheese, finely grated (reduced-fat if preferred), separated
2 eggs, plus 1 extra egg white

1. Heat oven to 375°F/190°C (Gas Mark 5).
2. In large saucepan, melt the fat and stir in the flour over very low heat.
3. When smoothly mixed, remove pan from heat and gradually blend in the milk. Return mixture to heat, and stir constantly to avoid burning as it thickens.
4. When you have a thick ball of mixture (a panada) that leaves the sides of the pan, remove from heat and cool slightly.
5. Stir in the cheese thoroughly, then beat in one egg yolk at a time.
6. Brush a high-walled casserole or soufflé dish thoroughly with fat.
7. Beat egg whites very stiff and fold into the mixture in three batches, using a metal spoon to 'cut' the whites in quickly but thoroughly.
8. Transfer mixture to dish and bake immediately for 30 minutes. Serve at once. If preferred, use three individual ovenproof dishes and bake for 15-20 minutes each.

Celery and Walnut Savoury

Serves 4

Good for people who like a nutty, crunchy texture. The celery and walnuts can be varied with other vegetables, such as fennel or parsnips, or other nuts.

Imperial (Metric)

½ oz (15g) butter, oil or high pufa margarine
1 large onion, finely chopped
2 sticks celery, finely chopped
½ teaspoon mixed dried herbs or 1½ teaspoons fresh chopped herbs
4 oz (115g) wholemeal breadcrumbs
1 orange, well-scrubbed in hot water
2 oz (55g) walnuts, chopped
1 egg, beaten
¼ teaspoon yeast extract

1. Set oven to 350°F/180°C (Gas Mark 4).
2. Heat fat in a thick-based pan and cook onion and celery gently for 10 minutes with lid on.
3. Mix with the herbs, breadcrumbs and finely grated rind of the orange.
4. Add walnuts, juice of the orange, egg and yeast extract.
5. Spread the mixture about ¾-inch (2cm) deep in greased baking tin, and cook for about 25 minutes. Serve cut in wedges like a cake.

Cheese Pudding

Serves 4

A bit like a soufflé, with less glamour but also less work.

Imperial (Metric)

4 oz (115g) wholemeal breadcrumbs
3 oz (85g) any hard cheese, finely diced
½ large onion, very finely chopped
2 eggs
¼ pint (140ml) skim milk
1 level teaspoon dry mustard
A large pinch of freshly ground black pepper
4 teaspoons lemon juice

1. Set oven to 375°F/190°C (Gas Mark 5).
2. Mix all the ingredients.
3. Pour into a greased casserole and bake for 30 minutes until golden.

Two-way Pizza

Serves 4

Scone dough can provide you with a pizza that's ready in under 30 minutes, while traditional yeast dough is still fairly quick. A good way of making pizza fun is to half-bake individual bases, rolled out and placed on baking sheets. Then let each of the family arrange their own choice of toppings on their own little base. Thank you, Zoë, for this idea.

Imperial (Metric)

Yeast dough base:

6 oz (170g) plain wholemeal flour
½ teaspoon micronized yeast
Large pinch of sea salt
1 teaspoon oil, preferably olive oil
4 fl oz (115ml) warm water
Pinch of raw cane sugar or honey
Large pinch of vitamin C powder

1. Mix all the ingredients, adding only enough of the water to make a soft dough. Knead for 6-8 minutes, then cover with upturned mixing bowl or polythene sheet for 10 minutes (or refrigerate until wanted).
2. Roll out without re-kneading to cover a greased and warmed pizza tin thinly. If possible, allow to sit, covered with cloth or polythene, for 10-15 minutes before topping.

Quick scone base:

6 oz (170g) plain wholemeal flour
Pinch of sea salt
¼ teaspoon bicarbonate of soda
½ teaspoon cream of tartar
2 tablespoons oil or high pufa margarine
Skim milk to mix

1. Sieve flour with salt, soda and tartar, returning bran left in sieve to the mix.
2. Fork in the fat, then enough milk to make a smooth dough.
3. Roll out thinly to cover a greased pizza tin.

Topping:

1 onion, finely chopped
1 teaspoon olive oil
7 oz tomatoes, sliced or 1 small tin of tomatoes
1 tablespoon tomato purée
½ teaspoon dried oregano or 1 teaspoon fresh chopped
Your choice of 3 oz (85g) sliced mushrooms; chopped green or red sweet pepper; 2 oz (55g) walnut pieces; 3 oz (85g) tuna — or some of all of these. 3 oz (85g) grated mature Cheddar cheese (reduced-fat type if wished)
Black olives to taste

1. Gently cook the onion in the oil for about 10 minutes until soft.
2. Add the tomatoes, tomato purée and oregano. Cook for 2 minutes gently.
3. Spread over pizza base. Sprinkle with mushrooms, pepper, walnut or tuna, then with the cheese and olives.
4. Bake for 10 minutes in oven pre-heated to highest temperature, then turn oven to 400°F/200°C (Gas Mark 6) for further 5 minutes for scone base, 10 minutes for yeast base.

Wholemeal Pasta

Serves 4. Illustrated opposite.

Can't be claimed to taste better or be healthier than bought wholewheat pasta, but is much, much cheaper.

Imperial (Metric)

8 oz (225g) plain wholemeal flour, strong
2 eggs, beaten
1 tablespoon olive oil
Cold water to mix

1. Sift the flour into a bowl. You can either add back bran left in the sieve or keep aside for another recipe.
2. Make a well in the centre and pour in the egg. With a wooden spoon, mix in the oil and form a soft dough. If necessary, add 1-2 tablepoons cold water.
3. Knead the dough for about 5 minutes. Cover and set aside for 30 minutes.
4. *For immediate use:* Roll out very thinly and use to make Pasta Roll or Lasagne: you don't have to boil the pasta before making up the recipe, provided the sauce mixture is fairly wet.
5. *For later:* Roll out without re-kneading as thinly as you can. Strong flour is more elastic, so better for this recipe. Using kitchen scissors, cut into thin sheets for lasagne, or ribbon noodles. Dry the shapes by placing on a wire rack for about 1 hour, or freeze fresh.
   Refrigerate fresh pasta until wanted, and don't keep for more than 2-3 days.
6. To serve, boil your largest saucepan of water. When bubbling vigorously, add the pasta and boil for 3-5 minutes until a piece tastes done, but *al dente*, that is, still has some bite. Drain, and serve with sauce.

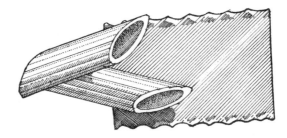

Opposite: Home-made Ribbon Noodles (above) with Pepper Sauce (page 33) *and* Falafal (page 36).

Opposite page 33: Raised Savoury Pie (page 40) *and* Cashew Nut Envelope (page 44).

Pepper Sauce for Pasta

Serves 4. Illustrated opposite page 32.

If available, use a mixture of green, red and yellow peppers for visual appeal.

Imperial (Metric)

1 tablespoon olive oil
1 medium onion, sliced
1 lb (450g) sweet peppers, sliced
1 large tin tomatoes or 14oz (400g) fresh sliced
Large pinch of oregano
Freshly ground black pepper to taste
Parmesan cheese to serve (optional)

1. Heat the oil in a large, thick-based saucepan. Add the onion, cover and cook over low heat for 10 minutes until soft but not coloured.
2. Add the peppers and continue cooking for about 5 minutes.
3. Add the tomatoes and oregano, and simmer for 10 minutes. Add black pepper to taste. When serving, sprinkle each portion with Parmesan cheese.

Tofu Pasta Sauce

Serves 4

Tofu — a low-fat beancurd made from soya beans — is available widely from health food stores. It has little flavour of its own, but absorbs the taste of the dish it is in, giving body and lots of protein.

Imperial (Metric)

2 onions, sliced
2 teaspoons oil
1 clove garlic, crushed
10 oz (285g) tofu (beancurd) cut in small cubes
12 oz (350g) mixed vegetables, chopped finely, e.g., carrots, mushrooms, courgettes,
    sweetcorn, cauliflower, broccoli
7 oz (200g) tomatoes, sliced or small can
1-2 tablespoons tomato purée
1 tablespoon soya sauce
2 teaspoons fresh chopped basil, if available
Freshly ground black pepper
2 tablespoons Parmesan cheese, grated

1. Cook onions in oil in a covered pan over very low heat for 10 minutes. Add garlic and cook for another 2 minutes, then tofu and cook for a further 2 minutes.
2. Add mixed vegetables, tomatoes and tomato purée. Bring mixture to the boil, cover and simmer for 10-15 minutes until vegetables are crunchy-tender. Add the soya sauce, basil and pepper.
3. Check seasoning. Serve sprinkled with Parmesan cheese.

Pasta Roll

Serves 4-5

A practical way of using freshly made pasta, because you don't have to cut it into shapes or boil it. This filling is ace for peanut fans, but you can easily ring the changes with other nuts or any other favourite pasta sauce.

Imperial (Metric)

¾ batch pasta dough (page 32)

Filling:

6 oz (170g) mushrooms, unpeeled and sliced
2 teaspoons oil
1 large onion, finely chopped
3 oz (85g) peanuts, toasted then ground
2 oz (55g) mature or reduced-fat Cheddar cheese, grated
2 tablespoons lemon juice
2 teaspoons soya sauce
2 spring onions, chopped
6 oz (170g) low fat soft cheese
1-2 tablespoons tahini (sesame spread), to taste
Parmesan cheese to serve

1. Cook the mushrooms and onion in the oil in a covered pan for 5 minutes. Remove lid and continue simmering for another 5 minutes.
2. Mix all the remaining ingredients. Add the mushrooms, onions and any pan juices. The mixture should be rather wet: if not, add a little water or skim milk.
3. Roll out the pasta dough very thinly on a clean, floured teacloth. Spread with the filling, raise cloth and roll up the dough into a long sausage shape.
4. Set oven to 375°F/190°C (Gas Mark 5). Tip 'sausage' into lightly greased ovenproof dish. Cover tightly with lid or foil. Bake for 50 minutes.
5. Serve sprinkled with Parmesan cheese.

Variations:

Traditional pasta sauces, such as cheese sauce, Bolognese or mushroom sauces can be rolled in the same way. For a simple lasagne-style dish, spread roll with lightly cooked spinach or mushrooms, then with cheese sauce, and pour over a small tin of tomatoes, mashed, before baking for 40 minutes uncovered.

Lentil Burgers

Makes 8, to serve 4 people

Season generously to taste. Serve in buns with burger trimmings and plenty of mild mustard.

Imperial (Metric)

½ large onion, finely chopped
1 stick celery, finely chopped
1 carrot, grated
1 teaspoon ground coriander
1 teaspoon ground cumin
1 bay leaf
2 tablespoons lemon juice
4 oz (115g) split red lentils, washed
Scant ½ pint (285ml) water
½ teaspoon Vecon
1 tablespoon chopped parsley
3 oz (85g) wholemeal breadcrumbs

To coat:

2-3 tablespoons plain wholemeal flour
1 small egg, beaten

1. In medium saucepan, bring the onion, celery, carrot, coriander, cumin, bay leaf, lemon juice, lentils, water and *Vecon* to the boil.
2. Reduce heat, cover and simmer for 25-30 minutes until lentils are tender and mixture dry.
3. Remove from the heat, extract bay leaf, add the parsley and about ⅓ of the breadcrumbs. Chill mixture for about 1 hour. Check seasoning.
4. Divide into 8 and shape into burgers. Heat grill.
5. Dip each burger in flour, then egg, then remaining breadcrumbs. Place on greased baking sheet. Grill for 3-4 minutes on each side. Serve with mild mustard.

Falafel

Makes 24 to serve 4-5 as a main course. Illustrated opposite page 32.

A Middle Eastern recipe with lots of flavour. Serve with (or in) wholemeal pitta bread with lots of salad and cubes of Cheshire cheese.

Imperial (Metric)

6 oz (170g) chick peas, dry weight
6 oz (170g) onion, finely chopped
2 teaspoons olive oil, cold-pressed
1½ teaspoons ground cumin
1½ teaspoons ground coriander
2 cloves garlic, crushed (optional, but traditional)
Juice of 1 lemon
2 tablespoons chopped parsley
Large pinch of freshly ground black pepper
Pinch of sea salt
4 oz (115g) wholemeal breadcrumbs
Plain wholemeal flour for coating

1. Soak chick peas overnight *or* bring to the boil in water to cover, simmer for 3 minutes, turn off heat and leave for 3 hours.
2. Liquidize soaked but raw chick peas in the minimum of cooking liquid to give a very solid purée.
3. Cook onion in the oil for 10 minutes, covered over low heat. Add the cumin, coriander and garlic, if using, and cook for further 2 minutes.
4. Add to the pan the lemon juice, parsley, pepper, salt and breadcrumbs. Remove pan from heat immediately. Stir in the chick pea purée.
5. Brush a large, thick-based frying pan with oil. Roll tablespoons of the mixture in a bowl of flour. Heat pan, then cook balls over lower heat for about 10-15 minutes on two sides, flattening slightly with spatula.

Quiche for all Seasons

Serves 4

Imperial (Metric)

6 oz (170g) wholemeal shortcrust pastry (page 25)
3 large eggs
½ pint (285ml) skim milk
1 tablespoon skim milk powder
¼ teaspoon freshly ground black pepper
4 oz (115g) mature or reduced-fat Cheddar cheese, grated

Filling:

Spring: 6 oz (170g) onions, chopped
Summer: 3 courgettes, in ¼ inch (½cm) slices
Autumn: 6 oz (170g) mushrooms, unpeeled and roughly chopped
Winter: 2 leeks, washed and finely sliced or chopped

1. Set oven to 350°F/180°C (Gas Mark 4).
2. Roll out pastry thinly on a sheet of polythene or foil to fit a 7 or 8 inch (18-20cm) flan tin with raised sides. Trim edge.
3. Cook your choice of filling in pan containing 1 teaspoon oil and a few tablespoons of water for about 8 minutes. (Omit water for mushrooms.) Cover pan tightly, then remove for further 2 minutes to let liquid evaporate.
4. Sprinkle flan base with chosen filling. In blender, combine eggs, milk, milk powder, pepper and cheese. Pour over filling.
5. Bake for 30-40 minutes, or until set but not hard.

Variations:
Fillings can be mixed in one quiche, with a neat wedge of each type or by stirring them together.
For a lower-fat quiche, use Yeast Pastry (page 26), and eat hot.

Savoury Crumble

A recipe for a thousand variations: you can 'crumble' almost any mixture of vegetables you have, and add cubes of cooked meat or cheese if wished.

Imperial (Metric)

Topping:

1½ oz (45g) high pufa margarine
3 oz (85g) plain wholemeal flour
1 oz (25g) wholemeal breadcrumbs
1 teaspoon fresh chopped herbs or ½ teaspoon dried herbs
Large pinch of freshly ground black pepper
Pinch of sea salt (optional)

Base:

1 oz (25g) high pufa margarine or butter
1 oz (25g) plain wholemeal flour
½ (pint (140ml) skim milk
1 lb (450g) lightly cooked vegetables, e.g. sliced courgettes, mushrooms, carrots, celery, swede, onions, leeks, beans
½ oz (15g) Parmesan cheese
Pinch of freshly ground black pepper

1. Set oven to 350°F/180°C (Gas Mark 4).
2. Make topping by rubbing fat into flour, then mixing in breadcrumbs, herbs and seasoning.
3. For the base, blend fat, flour and milk in liquidizer, transfer to small saucepan and heat gently, stirring constantly, until mixture thickens. Simmer for 4-5 minutes then stir in vegetables, Parmesan and pepper and transfer to casserole.
4. Sprinkle evenly with topping and bake for 30 minutes.

Harvest Pie

Just one of many savoury pies you can top with yeast pastry — or shortcrust if you prefer.

Imperial (Metric)

½ quantity yeast pastry (page 26)

Filling:

3 oz (85g) dried chestnuts, soaked in cold water overnight
1 large carrot, sliced
6 oz (170g) swede, in large dice
2 sticks celery, in ½ inch (1cm) lengths
3 medium onions, roughly chopped
½ teaspoon Vecon
1 cooking apple, diced
1 tablespoon lemon juice
2 oz (55g) wholemeal breadcrumbs

1. Bring soaked chestnuts to the boil covered with water. Reduce heat and cover pan. Simmer gently for about 40 minutes or until tender. Check level of water occasionally, adding more if chestnuts get dry.
2. Meanwhile, place all the vegetables in a large saucepan, adding ½ inch (1cm) depth of water. Stir in the *Vecon*, bring to the boil, cover and simmer for 15 minutes.
3. Stir in the apple, which you have tossed in the lemon juice (adding juice too), and the breadcrumbs.
4. When chestnuts are tender, drain and mix with the vegetables. Put the mixture in a lightly greased casserole.
5. Roll out the yeast pastry to cover pie. Cut decorative shapes with pastry trimmings, and make a hole in centre for steam to escape.
6. Heat oven to 425°F/220°C (Gas Mark 7). Brush pastry with egg retained from making pastry, and bake for 20 minutes.

Raised Savoury Pie

Serves 6-8. Illustrated opposite page 33.

Hot water crust pastry is very easy to make and work with, and has a slightly lower proportion of fat to flour than shortcrust. You can make many variations on the filling and decoration of these showpieces.

Imperial (Metric)

Hot water crust pastry:

¼ pint (140ml) water
4½ oz (125g) butter or solid vegetable fat or a mixture
12 oz (350g) plain wholemeal flour
Pinch of sea salt
Beaten egg to glaze

Filling:

8 oz (225g) potatoes, washed and peeled if old
1 onion, thinly sliced
1 teaspoon oil
8 oz (225g) cottage cheese
4 oz (115g) spinach, frozen in chunks, or 6 oz (170g) fresh, finely chopped
3 oz (85g) mature or reduced-fat Cheddar cheese
7 oz (200g) tomatoes, sliced or 1 small tin
1 teaspoon dried thyme or 2 teaspoons freshly chopped
2 tablespoons rolled oats
Large pinch of freshly ground black pepper

1. Boil the water and fat in large pan. Remove from heat, immediately tip in all the flour and the salt. Knead to make a soft dough, adding a little more very hot water if necessary.
2. On a floured worktop knead two-thirds of dough briefly to remove cracks, then place in well-greased 7-inch (18cm) diameter cake tin and pat out with hands to line base and sides. The pastry should be about ¼ inch (7mm) thick. Ideally, use a springform tin or one with a removable base. Otherwise, make a 'cradle' of two 4-inch (10cm) wide, long strips of greaseproof paper to put in the tin at right-angles, under the pie. These will enable you to lift it out easily. Grease these thoroughly too.
3. Boil or steam the potatoes for about 20 minutes until just tender. Drain, cut into slices.
4. Sauté the onion in the oil for 10 minutes, with the lid on. Mix with the potatoes and half the cottage cheese, spread evenly over base of pie.
5. Top with the spinach, followed by the hard cheese slices and remaining cottage cheese.

40

6. Mix tomatoes with the thyme, rolled oats and pepper, and spread over other fillings.
7. Set oven to 425°F/220°C (Gas Mark 7).
8. Roll out remaining pastry to make a lid for the pie. Make a cut in the centre to let steam escape, and use pastry trimmings to make decorations. (If you have some pastry left over, don't worry. This is preferable to making the pie pastry too thick. Roll it out, place in the centre a peeled, eating apple stuffed with dates, wrap and bake an apple dumpling for 25 minutes alongside the pie.)
9. Seal pie edges by pressing, and flute decoratively. Brush pie top with egg and bake for 20 minutes. Reduce heat to 375°F/190°C (Gas Mark 5) and bake for a further 30 minutes.
10.Carefully remove pie from tin, brush top and sides with egg and bake for further 10 minutes. Serve hot or cold.

Variations:
This pie sounds complicated, but as the pastry is easy and quick to make, it can be very practical for regular use. Other fillings could be: sliced boiled onions layered with bolognese sauce; hard-boiled eggs surrounded by spinach mixed with white sauce and flavoured with nutmeg; flakes of fish with cooked rice and mushrooms, moistened with white sauce.

This pie will take about 2 lbs (900g) filling, as described here. Seasoning should be generous, or the result will be bland. Use lemon juice, in place of salt, if you wish. The filling should not be wet, or the pie will sag when removed from tin.

Popovers

Makes 9

The nearest thing to a wholemeal Yorkshire pudding. Ideal for adding body to a vegetable casserole or salad meal.

Imperial (Metric)

2 large eggs
4 fl oz (115ml) skim milk
2 oz (55g) plain wholemeal flour

1. Set oven to 375°F/190°C (Gas Mark 5).
2. Place ingredients in blender, adding flour last. Blend for 45 seconds until smooth.
3. Grease 9 depressions on deep bun tin very thoroughly. Pour mixture into holes, filling just below rim.
4. Bake for 40-45 minutes. Serve immediately with savoury dishes or with stewed fruit.

Cheese and Tomato Gougère

Serves 4

This is a circle of soufflé-like choux pastry, with a savoury smooth filling of cheese and tomato. Use strong-flavoured cheese and plenty of mustard and pepper for a stronger-flavoured dish. Other fillings, such as pasta sauces, can be substituted.

Imperial (Metric)

3 oz (85g) plain wholemeal flour
¼ pint (140ml) water
2 oz (55g) high pufa margarine or *butter* or *a mixture*
2 eggs, beaten

Filling:

1 oz (25g) high pufa margarine or *butter* or *a mixture*
1 oz (25g) plain wholemeal flour
1 teaspoon dried mustard
½ pint (285ml) skim milk
3 oz (85g) well-flavoured Cheddar cheese or *reduced fat cheese, finely grated*
4 large tomatoes
Freshly ground black pepper to taste

1. Heat oven to 400°F/200°C (Gas Mark 6).
2. Sift flour, retaining bran left in the sieve to one side.
3. Boil water with fat, remove pan from heat and immediately tip in all the flour. Beat the mixture vigorously until it is smooth and leaves sides of pan clean. If necessary, return to gentle heat to reach this texture.
4. Still with pan off heat, beat in the egg a little at a time, making sure the mixture stays glossy and smooth.
5. Spoon mixture around the sides of a deep casserole dish and bake for 35 minutes until well-risen and crisp.
6. Meanwhile, make the filling by melting fat, then stirring in flour and mustard.
7. Remove pan from heat and blend in milk gradually and smoothly. (As an alternative to this method, blend flour, mustard, fat and milk in liquidizer, then carry on from here.)
8. Heat mixture gently, stirring continuously until sauce thickens. Add bran retained from sieving flour. Simmer mixture gently while you chop 3 of the tomatoes, add to the sauce with all but 1 tablespoon of the cheese. Add pepper and check seasoning.
9. When gougère is baked, pour sauce into centre, garnish quickly with remaining tomato and cheese, and serve without delay.

Savoury Bread and Butter Pudding

Serves 3-4

Homely but satisfying supper dish.

Imperial (Metric)

2 oz (55g) medium-fat curd cheese
1 oz (25g) butter, softened, or high pufa margarine
1 clove garlic, crushed (optional)
1 tablespoon chopped fresh parsley
4 thin slices wholemeal bread
3 eggs
Generous ½ pint (300ml) skim milk
6 oz (170g) finely chopped quick-cooking vegetables, such as courgettes, spring onions,
 sweetcorn, green or red pepper, young turnips, cucumber, broad beans etc.
Generous pinch of freshly ground black pepper
Pinch of sea salt (optional)
3 oz (85g) mature Cheddar cheese, grated*

1. Set oven to 400°F/200°C (Gas Mark 6).
2. Mash curd cheese, fat, garlic if using and parsley. Spread on one side of the bread slices.
3. Place half the bread, spread side down, in a small, greased ovenproof dish.
4. Beat together the eggs and milk, stir in pepper, salt if using and cheese.
5. Spread vegetables over bread slices, pour over half the egg mixture.
6. Top with remaining bread, followed by remaining egg and cheese mix.
7. Bake for 30-35 minutes.

*If wished, use reduced-fat Cheddar cheese.

Cashew Nut Envelopes

Makes about 6-7. Illustrated opposite page 33.

Savoury packets that are good for picnics, packed lunches or family meals. The filling can be varied.

Imperial (Metric)

1 quantity yeast pastry (page 26)

Filling:

1 onion, finely chopped
1 carrot, coarsely grated
4 oz (115g) swede or turnip, in very small slices
4 oz (115g) any other vegetables, e.g., mushrooms, leeks, fennel, celery, peas, green
*   beans, finely chopped*
2 teaspoons peanut or corn oil
2 teaspoons soya sauce
1 teaspoon dry sherry
1 teaspoon cornflour
4 tablespoons water
1 teaspoon vinegar
2 oz (55g) cashew nut pieces
A little beaten egg, to glaze

1. Heat oil in large, thick-based saucepan and turn onion in it over lowest heat. Cover and simmer for 5 minutes. Add carrot and other vegetables and continue for about 5 minutes more.
2. Mix soya sauce, sherry and cornflour to a smooth paste with a little of the water. Stir in remaining water and vinegar, and add this blend to the vegetables, stirring in. Simmer for 3-4 minutes.
3. Set oven to 400°F/200°C (Gas Mark 6). Roll out yeast pastry thinly.

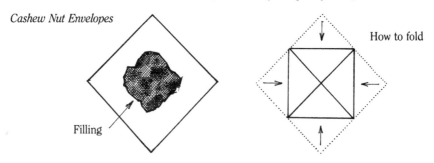

Cashew Nut Envelopes

Filling

How to fold

4. Toast cashew nuts in ungreased frying pan over low heat for about 3 minutes or until they colour slightly. Add to vegetables.
5. Cut pastry into squares about 5-inches (12cm) each side. Place each one on baking sheet, and fill centre generously with vegetable mix. Fold up like an envelope, bringing points to centre, overlapping.
6. Brush with egg, bake for about 20 minutes. Serve hot or warm if possible.

Variations:
Envelopes like these can be filled with many other mixtures, such as any pasta sauce; mushrooms and hard-boiled eggs in white sauce, with some sour cream or smetana stirred in if liked; or with fruit purée, made very thick.

Dumplings

Makes about 12

Imperial (Metric)

4 oz (115g) plain wholemeal flour
2 teaspoons baking powder
Pinch of sea salt (optional)
1 oz (25g) high pufa margarine or butter or a mixture
Good handful chopped fresh parsley or other herbs, such as chives, tarragon, thyme
1 egg, beaten
A little milk, to mix

1. Sift the flour with baking powder and salt if using.
2. Rub in the fat, stir in the herbs and egg and enough milk to make the mixture stick together.
3. Drop spoonsful of the mixture on to the top of a simmering casserole or soup and cook for about 10-12 minutes.

Note:
This is very similar to a scone mixture. You can make herb scones to go with your soup or casserole by adding a little extra milk to spare dough to make a very soft, sticky mixture. Pat balls into shape and bake on greased baking tin for 12 minutes in very hot oven.

Savoury Strudel

Serves 4

Once you've tried strudel dough, you'll wonder why you never made it before. You do need strong flour for this one. You can wrap many savoury fillings in this way, such as lightly-cooked Brussels sprouts with sweetcorn and prawns.

Imperial (Metric)

6 oz (170g) strong plain wholemeal flour
1½ tablespoons oil
1 small egg
A very little warm water, to mix

Filling:

12 oz (350g) low-fat curd cheese
6 oz (170g) sweetcorn or favourite cooked vegetable, chopped
2 oz (55g) walnuts or hazelnuts, toasted and chopped
2 tablespoons chopped parsley
Generous seasoning

1. Sieve the flour, whisk the oil with the egg and add to the flour.
2. Work together, then add a very little water to make a soft dough.
3. Knead on floured worktop just until it no longer sticks to hands or surface.
4. Cover with upturned mixing bowl and leave for 30 minutes.
5. Stretch a clean teacloth on worktop and sprinkle with flour. Place dough in the centre and roll out as thinly as possible. The dough will be elastic, and you can pull it out gently with your hands until it is almost thin enough to see through.
6. Spread with the mixed filling ingredients.
7. Grease a baking sheet and set oven to 450°F/230°C (Gas Mark 8).
8. Raise end of cloth nearest to you and roll up dough and filling like a roly-poly. Tip on to baking sheet.
9. Bake for 10 minutes, then reduce heat to 375°F/190°C (Gas Mark 5) for further 20 minutes or until lightly browned.

Savoury Strudel

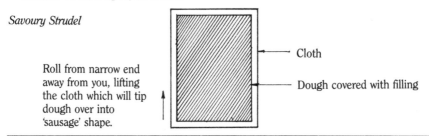

Roll from narrow end away from you, lifting the cloth which will tip dough over into 'sausage' shape.

Cloth

Dough covered with filling

5.
Desserts

Making puddings with wholemeal flour plus a low level of fat and sugar means you can eat and enjoy them without feeling you are hurting your health or your figure.

The recipes in this chapter are as good for you as a main dish, for instance. Naturally, if you eat large amounts of both main dish and dessert, you may end up with too many calories for the amount of energy which you as an individual require. In which case, you'll gain weight. But if you match solid desserts with light main courses, such as salads, and make full use of fruit desserts when eating a substantial main course, you'll keep the balance.

Wholemeal puddings have a good golden colour, nutty texture and lots of flavour. Because they're high in fibre (not only from flour, but often also from fruit), you'll tend to be satisfied with smaller portions.

Fruit Crumble

Serves 4

Always a favourite.

Imperial (Metric)

3 oz (85g) dates or sultanas, simmered for 10 minutes in water to cover, then puréed
1¼ lb (570g) prepared sweet fruit

Topping:

Crumble topping, as in Savoury Crumble, page 38, omitting herbs and adding
  1 oz (25g) sugar to the mixture

1. Set oven to 350°F/180°C (Gas Mark 4).
2. Place fruit in ovenproof dish, stirring the fresh and dried fruit purée together.
3. Spread the topping over evenly. Bake for 40-45 minutes.

Stuffed Apple Dumplings

Serves 4

Dessert apples are needed for this recipe: they keep their shape better during baking and, being sweeter, need no added sugar. You can wrap pears in the same way.

Imperial (Metric)

½ quantity yeast pastry (page 26)
4 medium dessert apples, peeled and cored
2 oz (55g) sultanas, soaked in boiling water for 5 minutes or 3 oz (85g) mild cheese, e.g., Cheshire, crumbled
2 teaspoons clear honey
1 teaspoon ground cinnamon

1. Set oven to 400°F/200°C (Gas Mark 6).
2. Roll out the pastry thinly — it will thicken slightly on baking.
3. Stuff the apples with the sultanas or cheese, and brush with the honey.
4. Cut pastry into four, and wrap apples up, with joints at bottom.
5. Use the pastry trimmings to cut decorative 'leaves' and place on top of apples. To get the best effect, stiffen this pastry slightly by kneading a little extra flour into it, and prop the leaves up with small balls of dough beneath them. Mark leaf 'veins' deeply with a sharp knife.
6. Brush apples with the egg reserved from making yeast pastry. Sprinkle with the cinnamon. Bake for 25-30 minutes.

Opposite: French Apple Tart (page 56) *and* Hazelnut Brown Bread Ice (page 55).

Plum Cobbler

Serves 4-5. Illustrated opposite.

Turns stewed fruit into something special. Much lower in fat than a shortcrust pastry pie, this goes well with a salad main course. Serve with real egg custard (see page 50).

Imperial (Metric)

1 lb (450g) plums
2 tablespoons honey (or less, to taste)

Scone Cobbler:

7 oz (200g) plain wholemeal flour
½ teaspoon bicarbonate of soda
1 teaspoon cream of tartar
2 oz (55g) high pufa margarine
¼ pint (140ml) skim milk
1 tablespoon honey

1. Place plums in casserole with the honey and a little water, and bake at 375°F/190°C (Gas Mark 5) for 20 minutes.
2. Meanwhile, sift flour, soda and cream of tartar, keeping back any bran left in sieve.
3. Mix in the margarine with a fork, then use fork to whisk the skim milk and honey together.
4. Add the liquid to the flour until you have a very soft dough.
5. Sprinkle retained bran on worktop and pat out dough ¾ inch (2cm) thick.
6. Cut rounds of dough. Take plum casserole from oven, and turn up heat to 425°F/220°C (Gas Mark 7).
7. Arrange scone rounds, overlapping, on top of the plums. Brush with milk. Bake for 10-15 minutes, until scones are firm.

Opposite: Apricot Cheesecake (page 57) *and* Plum Cobbler (above).

Egg Custard Sauce

As easily made as the cornflour variety, and much much nicer.

Imperial (Metric)

2 eggs
1 tablespoon skim milk powder
½ pint (285ml) skim milk
1-2 tablespoons honey, to taste
Few drops natural vanilla flavouring

1. Boil a saucepan of water on which a second saucepan will sit.
2. Blend the eggs, milk powder, milk and half the honey in liquidizer.
3. Pour into second saucepan, heat over simmering water, stirring constantly, until the mixture thickens. Do not let it boil or it will curdle.
4. Remove from heat, add the vanilla flavouring. Taste and add a little more honey if wanted.

Summer Pudding

Serves 4-5.

Traditionally made with redcurrants and other summer soft fruit, this can be made in winter with combinations such as plums, frozen raspberries and rhubarb.

Imperial (Metric)

1 lb (450g) fruit, trimmed and/or stoned
2 tablespoons water
Honey to taste — about 2 tablespoons
4-6 oz (115-170g) thin sliced wholemeal bread, with crusts removed

To serve:

4 oz (115g) extra fruit of same kind(s)

1. Heat the fruit in the water, covering pan tightly. If using soft fruit, cook just until juices run. If using harder fruit, chop before cooking and simmer until tender.
2. Sweeten to taste with the honey.
3. Line a small basin or bowl with the bread without any cracks.
4. Pour in the fruit. Cover with more trimmed bread to fit exactly.
5. Cover the pudding with a flat saucer that fits inside bowl or basin rim. Weight with heavy tin. Leave pudding in cool place overnight.
6. Turn out carefully on serving plate. If juice from fruit has not completely coloured pudding, stew a little of the extra fruit and 'colour in' gaps. Serve the extra fruit sliced or stewed next to the pudding.

Apple Charlotte

Serves 4-5.

Simple but good-looking enough for an occasion.

Imperial (Metric)

1 oz (25g) wholemeal breadcrumbs
2 tablespoons clear honey
1 lb (450g) eating apples, peeled and finely sliced or chopped
Juice and grated rind of 1 orange
5 slices from large wholemeal loaf, crusts removed
2 oz (55g) butter, melted or mix half-and-half with high pufa margarine

1. Set oven to 350°F/180°C (Gas Mark 4).
2. Mix the breadcrumbs, honey, apple slices, orange juice and orange rind and leave to sit while you prepare the charlotte.
3. Grease a small pudding bowl, 5-inch (12cm) cake tin or small loaf tin.
4. Brush a side of bread on both sides with the fat and trim to fit base of container you are using. Now trim more bread to fit sides neatly. Once you have cut them the right size, butter on both sides and fit into place. You should have enough bread left over to make a top.
5. Place the fruit in the container, pressing down well. Butter bread to make a lid.
6. Bake for about 45-55 minutes, until apples are tender. Turn out to serve hot or cold.

Variations:
Many other fruits can be used, either instead of or mixed with the apples. If using sourer fruit, such as blackcurrants, use a proportion of stewed dried apricots, chopped, to add sweetness.

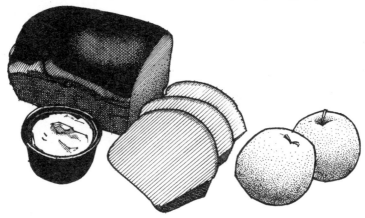

Plum Tart

Serves 8.

A kind of fruit pizza, with a light and tasty base.

Imperial (Metric)

5 oz (140g) plain wholemeal flour, preferably strong
½ teaspoon micronized yeast
1½ oz (45g) softened butter or *high pufa margarine* or *a mixture*
1 egg
Pinch of vitamin C powder
Warm water to mix

Topping:

1½ lb (680g) sweet small plums or *greengages*
2 tablespoons honey or *Demerara sugar*
1 teaspoon ground cinnamon
½ teaspoon mixed spice

1. Mix all the dough ingredients, adding enough water to give a soft mixture. Knead on floured worktop for 5-8 minutes. Cover with upturned mixing bowl.
2. Cut plums into neat halves and remove stones. Place in open baking dish, drizzle honey or sugar on top and bake for about 40 minutes, at 350°F/180°C (Gas Mark 4).
3. Without re-kneading dough, roll out on greased baking sheet to make a pizza-sized round. Arrange plum halves on top, if possible in neat rows, skin downwards.
4. Drizzle with remaining honey or sugar, then sprinkle with spices.
5. Allow to sit, covered with polythene, while you heat oven to 425°F/220°C (Gas Mark 7). Bake tart for 25 minutes, spooning over any juices from baking fruit half way through. Cover with foil if it over-browns.

Variations:
Other kinds of soft fruit can be used. Fruit like raspberries will only need pre-cooking until the juices run.

Steamed Honey and Lemon Pudding

Serves 6.

Really scrumptious. Serve leftovers, if any, as cake.

Imperial (Metric)

4 oz (115g) clear honey
6 oz (170g) plain wholemeal flour
1 teaspoon baking powder
3 oz (85g) high pufa margarine or 4 oz (115g) Gold
2 eggs
2 oz (55g) mixed peel, chopped
2 oz (55g) dried apricots, chopped
2 oz (55g) almonds, chopped
2 oz (55g) sultanas, washed
Juice of ½ lemon
About 2 tablespoons skim milk, to moisten

1. Boil a kettle of water.
2. Lightly grease a 2 pint (1.2 litre) pudding basin.
3. Beat all the ingredients together for 2 minutes, adding enough skim milk to make a soft, dropping consistency. Transfer to basin.
4. Cover with foil, making a pleat in the centre to allow for expansion. Tie tightly with non-synthetic string.
5. Place basin in large saucepan and add enough boiling water to come about two-thirds up sides of basin. Cover saucepan tightly, bring back to the boil. Simmer for 2 hours, adding extra boiling water if level drops lower than halfway up basin side.
6. To serve, run palette knife round pudding then turn out on heated plate. Serve with egg custard or jam sauce, made by gently heating no-added-sugar jam with enough water to make a pouring consistency.

Hazelnut Brown Bread Ice

Serves 4. Illustrated opposite page 48.

A crunchy cool taste to dress up fresh fruit.

Imperial (Metric)

2 oz (55g) hazelnuts, finely chopped
3 oz (85g) wholemeal breadcrumbs
2 oz (55ml) clear honey
10 fl oz (285ml) plain low fat yogurt
4 egg whites

1. In a thick-based, ungreased frying pan, stir nuts, crumbs and honey with a fork over a low heat for a few minutes until they brown slightly.
2. Cool while you beat the egg whites stiff.
3. Fold yogurt into crumb mixture.
4. Using a large metal spoon, fold egg whites in carefully, avoiding flattening the texture.
5. Freeze for 1½ hours or until wanted.
6. If freezing for later use, remove about 40 minutes before serving to allow to soften. Scoop into individual glasses and serve with a hazelnut on top, garnished with fresh fruit or small biscuits.

French Apple Tart

Serves 4. Illustrated opposite page 48.

Always makes a meal special. Double the size for a party piece.

Imperial (Metric)

Pastry:

½ teaspoon micronized yeast
3 oz (85g) plain wholemeal flour
1 egg, beaten
1½ fl oz (45ml) skim milk, just warmer than your finger
½ oz (15g) high pufa margarine
1 teaspoon honey

Filling:

2 oz (55g) dried apricots, washed
1 lb (450g) eating apples, washed
2 teaspoons honey
1 teaspoon cinnamon

To glaze:

About 2 tablespoons apricot jam

1. Simmer apricots in water to cover, with lid on, for 20 minutes.
2. Meanwhile, mix all pastry ingredients, retaining a very little of the egg for glazing. Knead on floured worktop for about 5 minutes. Cover with polythene bag or upturned mixing bowl.
3. Chop half the apples roughly and add to the apricot pan. There should be very little water in the mixture. After 8 minutes, remove from heat and stir in the honey and half the cinnamon. At this stage, you can either liquidize the mixture, or keep the apricots in pieces.
4. Roll out the dough without re-kneading to fit an 8-inch (20cm) flan tin. The pastry will be very thin: it will thicken on baking. Pour over the fruit mixture and smooth.
5. Set oven to 400°F/200°C (Gas Mark 6).
6. Slice remaining apples, unpeeled, very thinly. Arrange in overlapping lines to cover fruit mixture, working quickly so fruit does not discolour. If there is any delay, toss the apple slices in lemon or orange juice.
7. Sprinkle remaining cinnamon on top, cover whole tart loosely with foil. Bake for 20 minutes, then remove foil for further 10 minutes of baking.
8. Warm apricot jam to soften, then brush over apple but not pastry part of tart while still warm.

Apricot Cheesecake

Serves 5-6. Illustrated opposite page 49.

Very soft when just baked, serve this warm or cold, by which time it will have firmed up.

Imperial (Metric)

2 oz (55g) dried apricots
2 eggs, separated
8 oz (225g) low-fat soft cheese
1 tablespoon plain wholemeal flour
A few drops natural vanilla flavouring
1 tablespoon clear honey
2 oz (55g) sultanas, washed
2-3 tablespoons plain yogurt (you may need a little more)
Fresh fruit to garnish (optional)

Base:

2 oz (55g) wheatgerm, Grapenuts or similar crunchy cereal or crumbled sweet biscuits

1. In small saucepan, cover apricots with water, boil and drain. Re-cover barely with water, boil and simmer covered for 25 minutes.
2. Beat egg whites stiff.
3. Set oven to 350°F/180°C (Gas Mark 4).
4. In another large bowl, beat the soft cheese, flour, vanilla, egg yolks and honey together.
5. Sprinkle a small, deep-sided casserole, ungreased, with base.
6. Liquidize apricots with just enough cooking liquid to make a stiff purée. Add to the cheese mixture with the sultanas and enough yogurt to make a fairly wet mixture. Fold in the egg whites.
7. Pour mixture into prepared dish, bake for 25-30 minutes until almost firm. Turn oven off, leave door ajar and let cheesecake sit for about 30 minutes.
8. If wished, decorate top with rows of sliced fruit. Serve just warm or chilled.

Crêpes

Serves 4-5.

Think of crêpes more often: they are a convenient dessert which is quicker to make than you expect.

Imperial (Metric)

4 oz (115g) plain wholemeal flour
1 large egg or 2 small eggs
½ pint (285ml) skim milk
2 teaspoons oil

Fillings:

- *stewed fruit, or*
- *low-fat smooth soft cheese, mixed with washed raisins, a little vanilla essence and honey to taste, or*
- *low-fat smooth soft cheese sweetened to taste with honey, mixed with puréed fruit, such as raspberries, blackcurrants or mango, or*
- *no-added-sugar jam plus some chopped toasted nuts, or*
- *mincemeat (page 95) mixed with stewed apples*

1. Blend crêpe ingredients in liquidizer goblet.
2. Prepare filling.
3. Brush lightly with oil a thick skillet (preferably cast iron) and heat thoroughly.
4. Holding handle of skillet in one hand, swirl pan round to spread evenly the minimum of batter to cover base, poured from liquidizer goblet.
5. Reduce heat to medium and cook crêpe for about 1 minute until edges curl and bubbles break on surface. Turn, cook about 30 seconds.
6. If using immediately, tip each crêpe as made on to a warmed serving dish. You can fill one crêpe while the next cooks.
7. If using later, cool on wire rack so they don't overlap and stick together. Re-heat in hot skillet for less than a minute each. Store well-wrapped in foil or polythene to prevent drying out, in refrigerator or freezer. If freezing, one crêpe at a time can be removed and heated without thawing.
8. To serve, place filled crêpes in a lightly-oiled skillet to heat through over low heat, or wrap in foil and re-heat in oven for about 20 minutes at medium heat.

Apple Strudel

Serves 4.

Strong flour enables you to stretch the dough paper-thin, and the result is a favourite dessert or cake. Keep the apple slices very thin or the fruit won't cook through.

Imperial (Metric)

Studel dough, as for Savoury Strudel (page 46)

Filling:

1¼ lb (560g) eating apples, very thinly sliced
1 oz (25g) wholemeal breadcrumbs
2 oz (55g) currants or sultanas, washed
2 tablespoons lemon juice
2 tablespoons honey
2 oz (55g) high pufa margarine, melted
2 teaspoons cinnamon

1. Mix apples, breadcrumbs, dried fruit, lemon juice and honey.
2. Roll out strudel dough paper-thin on floured teacloth.
3. Set oven to 450°F/230°C (Gas Mark 8). Brush dough with melted margarine.
4. Spread apple mixture evenly over dough.
5. Sprinkle with most of the margarine, and half the cinnamon.
6. Raise end of cloth nearest to you and roll the dough and apples up into a 'sausage'. Tip on to a greased baking sheet.
7. Brush with remaining margarine, sprinkle with remaining cinnamon and bake for 10 minutes. Reduce heat to 350°F/180°C (Gas Mark 4) and cook for further 25 minutes, or until apples are tender when pierced with skewer.

6.
Cakes

Wholemeal flour is not just for breadmaking. Cakes made with it are less airy, but most people will find that they soon stop measuring the success of a cake by its height. Taste and texture are what matter.

Wholemeal flour is ideally suited to fruit cakes and gingerbread, where its ability to absorb more moisture during the making means that cakes stay deliciously moist.

You'll also be surprised to find how light and airy eclairs and other choux pastry dishes are with wholemeal: not just a better colour than ones made with white flour.

The nutty qualities of wholemeal flour can also improve certain dishes, such as the Apricot Slices on page 69, or Carob Brownies, on page 71.

Each recipe recommends whether wholemeal flour should be used as it is, or sieved (with the bran kept aside) to produce a lighter result. A good way of getting the best of both worlds is to use the retained bran to 'flour' the greased cake tin, and to sprinkle some on top of the cake before it goes into the oven. This means you still eat the fibre and the whole of the wheat grain, but the particles of bran aren't in the middle of the cake where they can impede rising. For ideas on what to do with any bran left over, see pages 107-109 in Chapter 11, High Fibre.

Once again, don't dismiss cakes as unhealthy stodge. Made this way, with less fat and sugar to provide 'empty' calories, and more high-food-value ingredients such as wheatgerm, soya flour, fruit, nuts and seeds, you don't have to feel bad about eating them.

Carrot and Walnut Cake

This recipe sounds too easy to be true, but the result is good. If you wish, turn it into a gâteau by cutting in half horizontally, then each half into two layers (alternatively, cut three horizontal layers) and sandwich with a double batch of American white frosting (page 116).

Imperial (Metric)

12 oz (350g) carrots, finely grated
4 oz (115g) walnuts, finely chopped
6 oz (170g) plain wholemeal flour
2 teaspoons baking powder
4 oz (115g) rolled oats
6 oz (170g) raisins, well washed
4 oz (115g) honey
3 eggs, beaten
6 tablespoons oil

1. Set oven to 350°F/180°C (Gas Mark 4).
2. Mix all the ingredients thoroughly.
3. Transfer mixture to a well-greased 7-inch (18cm) cake tin. Bake for about 65 minutes. Cool in the tin for about 15 minutes.

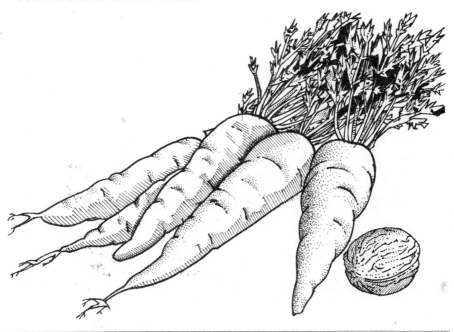

Yeast Fruit Cake

Illustrated opposite page 96.

No kneading is required for this simple cake. You can vary the flavour by changing the types of dried fruit and nuts used. Also good when slices are toasted.

Imperial (Metric)

3 oz (85g) dried apricots, chopped
4 oz (115g) sultanas
2 oz (55g) raisins
1½ teaspoons micronized yeast
10 oz (285g) plain wholemeal flour
2 heaped teaspoons mixed spice
1 heaped teaspoon ground cinnamon
3 oz (85g) nuts, toasted and chopped roughly
1 small orange, scrubbed and diced unpeeled
2 generous teaspoons vegetable oil
11 fl oz (310ml) water, just warmer than your finger
2 tablespoons honey

To Garnish:

½ oz (15g) sesame seeds or almond flakes

1. Place apricots, sultanas and raisins in saucepan, cover with water and bring to the boil. Drain through a sieve and leave to dry off (this process both cleans and warms them).
2. Mix yeast, flour, spice and cinnamon in a large bowl. Add the fruit and all the other ingredients. Stir vigorously for about 2 minutes.
3. The texture should be a very thick batter. Pour this into a very well-greased, warmed 7-inch (18cm) cake tin. Cover tin with polythene and leave in a warm, but not hot, place for about 1-1½ hours, until it is risen and bubbly.
4. Pre-heat oven to highest temperature. Sprinkle cake with sesame seeds or almond flakes. Bake for 10 minutes, then for 35-40 minutes at 400°F/200°C (Gas Mark 6) until cake begins to shrink from tin. Cool on rack.

Fruit Ring

With a dough similar to a French brioche, this is not a rich cake, but one with the interest of the fruit filling. For an even larger cake, keep the dough the same and double the amount of filling.

Imperial (Metric)

12 oz (350g) plain wholemeal flour
1 rounded teaspoon micronized yeast
Generous pinch of vitamin C powder
1 tablespoon honey
2 eggs, beaten (reserve small amount for glazing)
2 oz (55g) high pufa margarine or softened butter, or a mixture
About 6 fl oz (170ml) warm skim milk

Filling:
7 oz (200g) eating apple or pear, sliced or roughly chopped
1 tablespoon lemon juice
4 oz (115g) sultanas, or raisins, washed
1 tablespoon honey
2 oz (55g) dried pears, peaches or apricots, washed and roughly chopped
1 teaspoon ground cinnamon

1. Mix all the dough ingredients together, adding enough milk to make a soft dough. Knead on floured worktop for 5-8 minutes. Cover with upturned mixing bowl while you prepare filling.
2. Mix all the filling ingredients.
3. Without re-kneading dough, place on large greased baking sheet and roll out to a circle about 20-inches (50cm) across.
4. Spread with filling, leaving about a 4-inch (10cm) border of dough bare.
5. With scissors, cut border from edge to filling into 1-inch (2.5cm) strips.
6. Plait these loosely in groups of 3 and fold to cover, covering filling.
7. Brush ring with reserved egg and cover for 20 minutes. Heat oven to 400°F/200°C (Gas Mark 6) and bake for 30 minutes.

Variations.
Many other combinations of fruit and spice can be used.

Fruit Ring

Filling

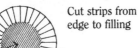

Cut strips from edge to filling

Fold to centre, plaiting

Fold plaits to centre over filling

Nut and Apple Slices

Another very moist fruit-cum-cake with an unconventional texture, and good taste.

Imperial (Metric)

8 oz (225g) thick apple purée, made with dessert apples stewed in very little water,
*   unsweetened, with 1 tablespoon lemon juice*
4 tablespoons clear honey
2 oz (55g) high pufa margarine
4 oz (115g) plain wholemeal flour
1½ teaspoons baking powder
¼ teaspoon ground cloves
½ teaspoon ground cinnamon
¼ teaspoon ground nutmeg
2 oz (55g) sunflower seeds, lightly toasted
2 oz (55g) hazelnuts, lightly toasted and roughly chopped

1. Set oven to 350°F/180°C (Gas Mark 4).
2. Cool the apple purée. Cream the honey and margarine thoroughly, then add purée.
3. Sift the flour, baking powder and spices. Stir in the nuts, then the apple mixture.
4. Grease a large loaf tin and add the mixture. Bake for 45 minutes. Cut into bars to serve.

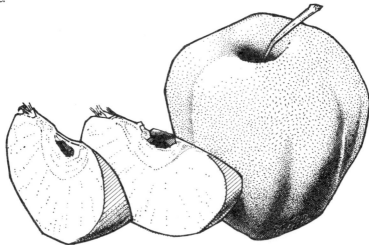

Opposite: Apricot Slices (page 69) *and* Carob Brownies (page 71).

Overleaf: English Muffins (page 76) *and* Pitta Bread with Salad (page 75); *and* Chelsea Buns (page 70) *and* Very Rich Plumcake (page 91).

Profiteroles and Eclairs

Makes 12 eclairs or profiteroles, to serve 4. Illustrated on front cover.

Beautifully light and airy. Not low-fat, but you rarely eat a large number of these, do you?

Imperial (Metric)

¼ pint (140ml) water
2 oz (55g) high pufa margarine
3 oz (85g) plain wholemeal flour
Pinch of sea salt (optional)
2 eggs, beaten

Topping:

1 carob bar, preferably no-added-sugar, melted in top of double saucepan with a knob of butter or high pufa margarine

1. Set oven to 400°F/200°C (Gas Mark 6).
2. Boil the water and fat together. Meanwhile, sift the flour with the salt if using. Return bran in sieve to flour.
3. When water mix boils, take pan off heat and immediately tip in all the flour at once. Beat vigorously with a wooden spoon until the mixture forms a smooth ball that leaves the sides of the pan clean. If it doesn't, beat over a low heat for a minute or two until it does.
4. Let the mixture cool for 10 minutes or so. Beat in the eggs a little at a time, making sure the mixture is smooth again after each addition.
5. Transfer to piping bag if making eclairs. If you don't have a special bag and nozzle, place in clean polythene bag and snip small hole across one corner. Pipe lengths on to greased baking sheet or eclair tin. To make profiteroles or choux buns, pipe balls of desired size or spoon out with teaspoon or tablespoon.
6. Bake for 20-25 minutes, remove from oven, make slit down side to let steam escape and return to oven. Turn off heat, but leave for a few minutes to crisp.
7. When cool, dip in melted carob from a bar (preferably no-added-sugar variety), and fill with crème fraîche or crème pâtissière (see Glazes and Fillings, page 116).

Variation:
For less fat, replace margarine with same weight of *Gold* low-fat spread and decrease amount of flour to 2½ oz (70g).

Opposite: Wholewheat Bagels (page 79).

Date and Walnut Tea Bread

A plain and tasty tea bread that's particularly nice when slices are toasted. Stale cake can be cut in slices and baked for about 30-40 minutes at 325°F/170°C (Gas Mark 3) on a baking sheet, or until cooked through but not hard. They will crisp on cooling into tasty rusks.

Imperial (Metric)

8 oz (225g) plain wholemeal flour
2 teaspoons baking powder
2 oz (55g) walnuts, chopped
6 oz (170g) stoned dates, chopped
3 tablespoons honey
1 large egg
¼ pint (140ml) skim milk
1 tablespoon lemon juice
1-2 tablespoons no-added-sugar apricot jam, to glaze

1. Set oven to 350°F/180°C (Gas Mark 4).
2. Sieve flour and baking powder together. Stir in the walnuts and half the dates.
3. Liquidize remaining dates with the honey, egg and skim milk.
4. Mix wet and dry blends, and stir in the lemon juice. Add a very little extra milk, only if needed, to make a dropping consistency.
5. Transfer mixture to a greased 6-inch (15cm) cake tin. Bake for about 50 minutes. Cool on wire rack and brush top and sides with apricot jam.

Sesame Bars

Makes about 12

If you don't like sesame, substitute chopped nuts, sunflower seeds or poppy seeds. The mixture in the middle looks very thin when raw, but works out fine.

Imperial (Metric)

2 oz (55g) sesame seeds
2 oz (55g) plain wholemeal flour
½ teaspoon baking powder
½ teaspoon ground cinnamon
10 allspice berries, crushed
½ teaspoon ground nutmeg
2 eggs
4 tablespoons honey
6-8 teaspoons sesame oil

1. Set oven to 350°F/180°C (Gas Mark 4).
2. Toast sesame seeds by stirring in thick-based, ungreased frying pan over low heat for 3-4 minutes, until they start to jump. Grind in coffee mill or food processor.
3. Sift the flour, baking powder and spices. Whisk together the eggs, honey and oil, and add to flour mix to make a batter.
4. Oil a sponge tin and sprinkle with half the sesame seeds. Pour the batter on top, then sprinkle with remaining seeds and press in lightly with fork.
5. Bake for 20 minutes. When almost cool, cut into bars.

Scotch Pancakes or Drop Scones

A popular and very quick recipe that's equally useful at breakfast time, tea time or as a snack. If you want a savoury topping, omit the honey from the recipe.

Imperial (Metric)

4 oz (115g) plain wholemeal flour
¼ teaspoon bicarbonate of soda
½ teaspoon cream of tartar
1 egg
1 tablespoon honey (optional)
Pinch of sea salt (optional)
Skim milk to mix, about ¼ pint (140ml)

1. Place all the ingredients in liquidizer and blend until smooth. Alternatively, sift flour, soda and tartar, beat in the egg and whisk the honey and salt, if using, with the milk. Add milk in two batches, to make a thick batter.
2. Heat a thick-based frying pan or griddle and brush lightly with fat.
3. Over low heat, drop spoonfuls of batter to make discs about 2-inches (5cm) across. Cook for about 1½ minutes on each side; it is time to turn the pancakes when bubbles appear and break on top.
4. Transfer cooked pancake to the folds of a clean teacloth. This keeps them soft by preventing steam escaping, as well as keeping them warm.

Variations:
Add ½ teaspoon mixed spice, some sultanas or a finely chopped eating apple to the batter (or all three).

Super-Moist Fruit Loaf

You'll sigh at the solid texture of this — but it tastes delicious.

Imperial (Metric)

8 oz (225g) apples, washed and chopped roughly, but not peeled
8 oz (225g) other seasonal fruit, e.g., plums
3 oz (85g) high pufa margarine
2 oz (50ml) clear honey
1 egg, beaten
2 oz (55g) chopped nuts
4 oz (115g) sultanas, washed
4 oz (115g) wholemeal flour
4 oz (115g) wholemeal breadcrumbs
1 teaspoon baking powder
½ teaspoon ground cinnamon
½ teaspoon ground nutmeg
½ teaspoon mixed spice

1. Stew fruit in 3 fl oz (85ml) water for 10 minutes. Remove stones if applicable, then liquidize fruit in cooking liquid. Cool a little. Set oven to 350°F/180°C (Gas Mark 4).
2. Cream margarine with honey, then beat in egg, followed by fruit purée, nuts and sultanas. Sieve flour with baking powder and spices, stir in breadcrumbs, then mix quickly but thoroughly with fruit mix.
3. Pour into a well-greased large (800g) loaf tin and bake for 1 hour. Cool on a rack.

Bread Pudding

Don't wait until you have some stale bread!

Imperial (Metric)

8 oz (225g) wholemeal bread, which can be stale or not
½ pint (285ml) skim milk
4 oz (115g) any mixture of currants, sultanas and raisins, washed
3 tablespoons high pufa margarine or softened butter
1 tablespoon honey
1 tablespoon mixed spice
1 teaspoon ground nutmeg
1 teaspoon lemon juice
2 teaspoons finely grated rind of well-scrubbed orange or lemon
1 egg, beaten

1. Set oven to 350°F/180°C (Gas Mark 4).
2. Soak the bread in the milk, squeezing mixture through your fingers until it is smooth.
3. Mix in all the other ingredients except for half the nutmeg.
4. Transfer to greased baking dish so mixture is at least 1¼-inches (3cm) deep. Sprinkle with remaining nutmeg and bake for 45-55 minutes until just set.

Fruit Slices

Illustrated opposite page 64.

Good as a dessert as well as a rather gooey cake.

Imperial (Metric)

Filling:

6 oz (170g) dried apricots, peaches or *pitted prunes, or a mixture*
2 tablespoons rolled oats

Base and topping:

2 oz (55g) wheatgerm
½ oz (15g) soya flour
2 oz (55g) plain wholemeal flour
1 tablespoon honey
1 oz (25g) high pufa margarine
2 tablespoons vegetable oil

To decorate:

½ oz (15g) sesame seeds or *flaked almonds*

1. Boil dried fruit, covered with water. Drain. Cover barely with fresh water, boil. Cover and simmer for about 25 minutes until tender.
2. Set oven to 350°F/180°C (Gas Mark 4).
3. Mix all the base ingredients and press half into base of greased sandwich tin. Bake for 8 minutes.
4. Liquidize fruit in enough of its cooking water to give a very thick purée. Add the oats to the blender.
5. Pour the mixture over the baked base, top with remaining mixture, pressing it firmly into the fruit with back of spoon. Sprinkle with sesame seeds or almonds.
6. Bake for 20 minutes, cool in the tin.

Chelsea Buns

Makes about 12. Illustrated between pages 64 and 65.

Worth doubling up the recipe and making a large batch, because you can freeze any you want to keep. Separate before freezing and you'll be able to take out one or more as needed, and warm them without the need to thaw, by grilling under moderate heat for a few minutes.

Imperial (Metric)

1 teaspoon micronized yeast
8 oz (225g) plain wholemeal flour
1 teaspoon mixed spice
Pinch of sea salt (optional)
1 teaspoon grated rind from well-scrubbed lemon
Pinch of vitamin C powder
4 oz (115ml) skim milk
1 oz (25g) high pufa margarine or butter, or mixture
2 teaspoons honey
1 egg, beaten

Filling:

4 oz (115g) mixture of currants and raisins, well-washed
½ oz (15g) high pufa margarine or softened butter
2 tablespoons honey

1. Mix first six ingredients in a warmed bowl.
2. Gently heat milk, fat and honey until the milk is just warmer than your finger. Stir into flour mixture with the egg, then knead dough on a floured worktop for 5-8 minutes.
3. Cover with upturned mixing bowl. Warm the fat and half the honey slightly for filling.
4. After dough has sat for a few minutes, roll out to a rectangle about 12×9-inches (30×23cm), with the narrower side facing you. Brush the dough with all the melted fat and honey mixture, then sprinkle with the dried fruit, pressing in lightly with the rolling pin.
5. Grease and warm a Swiss-roll tin, or something similar with slightly raised sides.
6. Roll up dough very loosely from the narrow end away from you.
7. Using your sharpest knife, cut the 'sausage' in half, then quarters, then each quarter into three to make 12 slices.
8. Place on baking tin, shaping them into squares with your fingers. They should not touch, but be close enough so they will join as they rise, with this and the sides of the tin keeping the traditional square shapes.
9. Cover loosely with polythene and leave to rise for 1-1½ hours. Heat oven to maximum, and when buns are puffy, bake for 5 minutes.

10. Reduce oven heat to 400°F/200°C (Gas Mark 6) and bake for a further 10 minutes. Meanwhile, slightly warm remaining honey. Remove from oven and brush with honey.

Carob Brownies

Makes about 15 slices. Illustrated opposite page 64.

Gooey and treacly, the thinking eater's answer to the usual heart-stoppingly rich American brownie recipe.

Imperial (Metric)

6 tablespoons vegetable oil
6 tablespoons clear honey
4 tablespoons molasses or black treacle
2 large eggs
½ teaspoon natural vanilla essence
4 oz (115g) plain wholemeal flour
1 teaspoon baking powder
1 oz (25g) carob powder
4 oz (115g) wheat germ
2 oz (55g) walnuts, roughly chopped
4 tablespoons skim milk

1. Set oven to 325°F/170°C (Gas Mark 3).
2. Beat the oil, honey and molasses until creamy, then beat in the eggs and vanilla.
3. Sieve the flour with the baking powder and carob, stir in the wheatgerm.
4. Add the walnuts and milk, then mix with oil blend. The mixture should be a thick batter.
5. Grease a baking tin with sides at least 1-inch (2.5cm) deep. Pour in mixture, which ideally should be ¾-inch (2cm) deep. Bake for 25-30 minutes until firm.
6. Cool in tin, cutting into slices while warm.

Variation:
Omit carob powder for plain brownies, or add 1 teaspoon ground ginger to the flour.

Almond Parkin

A traditional treacly parkin gingerbread with oatmeal.

Imperial (Metric)

6 oz (170g) molasses
8 oz (225g) plain wholemeal flour
2 oz (55g) fine or medium oatmeal
2 oz (55g) wholemeal breadcrumbs
2 teaspoons baking powder
2 teaspoons ground ginger
1 teaspoon mixed spice
2 oz (55g) high pufa margarine
3 oz (85g) sultanas, washed
½ pint (285ml) skim milk
2 oz (55g) almonds, roughly chopped

1. Set oven to 350°F/180°C (Gas Mark 4). Grease a large loaf tin.
2. Warm the molasses in a large saucepan.
3. Remove from heat, add all the remaining ingredients except almonds and mix well. Add a little extra milk if necessary to reach a dropping consistency.
4. Transfer to loaf tin. Sprinkle with the almonds. Bake for 50-60 minutes, or until skewer comes out clean. Cool in tin.

7.
Bread

Don't be put off baking your own bread because you see plenty of wholemeal bread in shops, and think you don't have time to make your own. The bread you make yourself still tastes far better, and it's never been easier to do. Just look how short the basic recipe is — and how quick. You are only 'working' for 10 minutes of that time. That's the chance for some therapeutic kneading of the dough — a great way of relaxing, combined with some excellent exercise for flabby upper arms!

Once you get into the habit of baking bread, you realize that you can be as casual with the recipes and dough as you want, and still turn out tasty loaves confidently.

Bread you want to keep can be frozen when fully cooled for up to three months. By slicing before freezing, you can take out as many pieces as you want and warm under grill, without having to wait for a whole loaf to thaw.

A 1½ kilo bag of flour will make five small loaves, or two large ones plus some rolls. So baking bread still saves a good deal of money. Small loaves are easier to bake through than large ones, which need roughly 15 minutes more baking. Rolls are quickest, as they rise faster and bake in 12 to 15 minutes.

A useful tip in all yeast baking is that people tend to make the dough a little dry and, by doing so, prevent it rising fully — so their bread is a little too solid for their liking. Dry dough may be less sticky when you start kneading, but quickly becomes too stiff. Aim for a soft dough, adding a little more warm water as you knead (by rinsing your hands in warm water, for instance, from time to time) to maintain a soft texture.

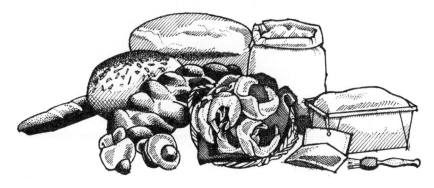

Wholemeal 90-minute Bread

A reliable, one-rising, easy-to-handle recipe, which makes 2 small loaves plus a few rolls. Double the quantity if wished.

Imperial (Metric)

1½ lbs (680g) plain wholemeal flour
1 teaspoon sea salt
1 teaspoon honey
1 tablespoon oil, margarine or softened butter
1 sachet micronized yeast
¼ teaspoon vitamin C powder
¾ pint (425ml) hand-warm water (110°F/43°C)

1. Mix all the ingredients in warmed bowl, adding a little more water if necessary to make a soft dough.
2. Knead well for about 7 minutes.
3. Cover with upturned mixing bowl or polythene while you warm and grease two 1 lb (500g) loaf tins or a large baking sheet.
4. Shape dough either into two loaves or into rolls, or a mixture. To make a neatly shaped tin loaf, use a rolling pin to flatten 1 lb (450g) dough into a rectangle the same width as the loaf tin, and three times as long as the narrow side of the tin. Fold the dough ends in to overlap, loosely, and place, join downwards, in the greased tin, or on baking sheet. After shaping two loaves, you will have enough dough left to make some rolls. See opposite for ideas on fancy roll shapes (illustrated opposite page 80).
5. Cover tins loosely with polythene, and let stand at room temperature or in a slightly warmer place such as an airing cupboard, for about 40 minutes, until dough has doubled in size.
6. Heat oven to maximum temperature before putting bread in. Bake loaves for 10 minutes, then reduce heat to 400°F/200°C (Gas Mark 6) for further 20-25 minutes. Bake rolls for 10-15 minutes at top heat.
7. If bread sounds hollow when based is tapped, and does not 'sing' when you put your ear to it, it is done. Cool on wire rack.

Shapes for Loaves or Rolls

Plait: divide dough into three, use palms of hands to make three long strands. Plait loosely, to allow room for rising. This is easiest done on baking sheet.

Cottage: roll balls of dough to desired base size and place on baking sheet. Roll a ball half as big as the first to top each, and place squarely on top. Make the rounds rather high: they will tend to sink as they expand. Dip a wooden spoon handle into flour and plunge through top and base.

Bloomer: roll dough into a long, round 'sausage'. Cut diagonal slashes across the top with a sharp knife before proving.

Crescent rolls: roll dough into large circle on baking sheet. Cut into 8 segments. Roll each loosely from wide end towards centre, so that last corner ends up on top. Bend the roll to make a crescent.

Cloverleaf rolls: make small balls of dough, and place three close but not touching on baking sheet. If liked, add a dough 'stem'.

Letter rolls: using a sharp knife or scissors, cut out letters. Decorate with leaves cut with sharp knife and marked with a knife.

Parkerhouse rolls: form a ball of dough, flatten slightly, and make a deep cut almost through the dough about a third from one end. Lift dough, and place on baking sheet upside down, pushing the two sections slightly together.

Knots: using palms of hands roll dough into a long thin sausage. For each sausage, fold a 12-inch (30cm) length of dough into two, and loosely twist them round each other a few times. Bring the ends together to form a knot.

Tree rolls: use scissors to cut out trees. Snip lightly at top of tree to form 'branch' markings.

Double S rolls: make a very thin sausage of dough, and form into spirals on baking sheet. Allow plenty of space between rings or dough will lose its distinctive shape.

Pitta breads: Roll 2 oz (55g) balls of dough into thin ovals. Bake for 10-15 minutes then wrap immediately in a tea towel to keep the steam in and bread soft. (Illustrated on back cover.)

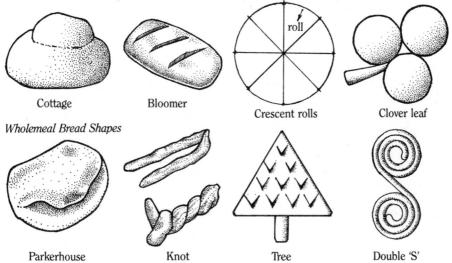

Cottage   Bloomer   roll / Crescent rolls   Clover leaf

Wholemeal Bread Shapes

Parkerhouse   Knot   Tree   Double 'S'

Toppings and Glazes

For a shiny finish, brush loaves or rolls with beaten egg, mixed with a very little water.

For a crisper crust, place a roasting tin of water in oven under bread shelf when you turn oven on.

For floury rolls, brush bread with milk and sprinkle with flour.

Rolled oats, sesame seeds, sunflower seeds, poppy seeds, wheat bran flakes, or chopped peanuts will add variety of appearance and flavour.

English Muffins

Makes 10. Illustrated on back cover.

You rarely see these in Britain! However, the Americans think they are English, and they are very tasty. You do need a really thick, ideally cast iron, skillet or griddle.

Imperial (Metric)

8 oz (225g) plain wholemeal flour
Good pinch of sea salt
1 teaspoon micronized yeast
Pinch of vitamin C powder
1 egg, beaten
½ oz (15g) high pufa margarine or melted butter
¼ pint (140ml) skim milk, just warmer than your finger
Oil for cooking

1. Mix all the ingredients except the oil for cooking. Turn this very soft dough onto a floured worktop and knead for 5 minutes until elastic.
2. Divide into 10 pieces. Knead each a little with palm of hand, and shape into a ball. Place them on warmed, greased baking sheet with some room to spread. Flatten with palm of hand to about 3-inches (8cm) across.
3. Leave for about 30 minutes or until risen.
4. Heat a thick-based skillet well and brush lightly with oil. Reduce heat a little. Cook muffins in batches, reducing heat after 30 seconds, for about 5 minutes on each side. Cool on rack. Serve split with savoury or sweet fillings.

Staffordshire Oatcakes

Makes 6 large oatcakes.

Not the crisp Scottish oatcake, but a large, floppy oat pancake to enjoy hot, under or beside any savoury; toasted with a savoury or sweet topping; or my favourite, with a thin omelette sandwiched between 2 oatcakes. These could be described as a Midlands tortilla.

Imperial (Metric)

4 oz (115g) plain wholemeal flour
4 oz (115g) fine or medium oatmeal
1 teaspoon micronized yeast
½ pint (285ml) boiling water
¼ pint (140ml) cold skim milk
Pinch of sea salt (optional)
Pinch of vitamin C powder

1. Mix all the ingredients, adding the boiling water to the skim milk before stirring into dry ingredients.
2. Cover bowl or jug with polythene and leave in warm place for about 40 minutes.
3. Heat a thick-based frying pan or griddle. Brush very lightly with oil.
4. Pour from the jug or bowl a small amount of batter, swirling the pan to spread thinly. These pancakes are not paper-thin like crêpes, but excess butter will make them stodgy. Pour any excess batter back into rest.
5. Over medium heat, cook for about 1-2 minutes until bubbles burst on surface, then for 1 minute on other side. Stack to cool: they don't tend to stick.
6. Store covered in refrigerator for up to 4 days. Re-heat under grill or in barely oiled pan for 1-2 minutes.

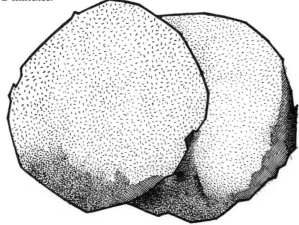

Little Cheese Squares

Makes about 15. Illustrated inside front cover.

Good for lovers of toasted cheese sandwiches.

Imperial (Metric)

12 oz (350g) plain wholemeal flour, preferably strong
1 generous teaspoon micronized yeast
1 teaspoon dry mustard
Pinch of sea salt (optional)
Pinch of vitamin C powder
8 fl oz (225ml) water just warmer than your finger
6 oz (170g) mature Cheddar or reduced fat cheese, grated
½ teaspoon dry sage, powdered

1. Mix ingredients down to the water into a soft dough. Knead on floured worktop for about 5 minutes, adding a little more warm water if the mixture gets stiff or dry.
2. Cover with upturned mixing bowl and leave for a few minutes.
3. Roll out without re-kneading into a rectangle about 12×9 inches (30×23cm). Sprinkle half the cheese and sage over two-thirds of dough. Fold third without cheese over, then this double thickness over the final third.
4. Turn 90 degrees, roll out to rectangle again and repeat, retaining a handful of the cheese. Fold again.
5. Cut into 16 squares. Place on warmed, greased baking sheet with some room to spread. Cover loosely with polythene and leave in warm place for about 1 hour.
6. Set oven to 425°F/220°C (Gas Mark 7). Brush baps with milk, then sprinkle with remaining cheese. Bake for 15 minutes. Serve hot, split open and filled with cottage cheese and cress.

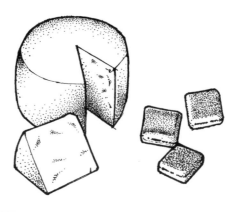

Bagels

Makes 25. Illustrated opposite page 65.

A Jewish tradition — which a witty American bakery described as 'Holey rolls' — this always proves a winner with small children.

Imperial (Metric)

1 lb (450g) plain wholemeal flour
¼ teaspoon vitamin C powder
1½ teaspoons micronized yeast
4 tablespoons oil
1 egg, reserving a little for glazing
½ teaspoon sea salt (optional)
½ pint (285ml) warm mixture of skim milk and water

1. Mix all the ingredients, adding extra liquid if necessary to make a soft dough.
2. Knead on floured worktop for 5-8 minutes.
3. With palms of hands, roll pieces of dough into long 'sausages'.
4. Cut lengths about 5-inches (12cm) long and pinch ends together to make rings. Place on greased and warmed baking sheet, cover with cloth or unprinted polythene and leave for 30-40 minutes to rise.
5. Set oven to highest temperature. Boil a large, wide container of water.
6. When water is simmering drop a few bagels at a time, turning after about 45 seconds, then removing and draining before returning to baking sheet. They will be swollen and puffy.
7. Brush with reserved egg and bake for 15-20 minutes. If liked, sprinkle with sesame, poppy, caraway or linseeds before baking.

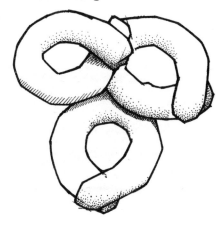

Swedish Rye Bread

Makes 1 large loaf. Illustrated opposite.

Completely different from ordinary bread, this is full of flavour. The longer fermentation period is used to bring out the distinctive taste.

Imperial (Metric)

8 fl oz (225ml) brown ale
6 oz (170g) wholemeal rye flour
1 teaspoon caraway or fennel seeds
14 oz (400g) plain wholemeal flour
½ teaspoon sea salt (optional)
2 teaspoons vegetable oil
1 tablespoon molasses
2 teaspoons micronized yeast, or 1 sachet
1 good teaspoon finely grated rind of scrubbed orange
¼ pint (140ml) water or skim milk

1. Heat the beer to lukewarm and stir in the rye flour. Cover and leave for 12-48 hours.
2. When ready to make bread, toast caraway or fennel seeds in thick-based, ungreased frying pan over low heat for 2-3 minutes, then grind in coffee mill or with pestle and mortar.
3. Mix all the ingredients together and stir thoroughly. Knead on floured worktop for 5 minutes, adding a little warm water if mixture seems stiff. Cover mixture with polythene bag or upturned mixing bowl and leave 1 hour.
4. Re-knead briefly and shape into a high lozenge. Place on greased, warmed baking sheet. Cover loosely again, let rise about 1 hour. Slash top decoratively if wished.
5. Pre-heat oven to 400°F/200°C (Gas Mark 6). Bake for about 40 minutes, or until it stops 'singing' when you put your ear to it. Cool on wire rack.

Opposite: Swedish Rye Bread (above) *and* Fancy Rolls (page 75).

Sourdough Bread

Makes 1 loaf.

If you like the distinct tangy-sour flavour of many north European breads, this is a way of getting it. The texture is very solid. If this doesn't suit you, go as far as point 2, then add the mixture to a conventional bread dough with yeast.

Imperial (Metric)

Stage 1:

1 cup cooked rice, porridge or other grain or of plain wholemeal flour
Sufficient mineral water to make a thick batter

Stage 2:

About 12 oz (350g) plain wholemeal flour
½ teaspoon sea salt (optional)
3 teaspoons oil or other fat
1 tablespoon linseed, poppy seed, caraway seed or sesame seed (optional)

1. If using cooked grain, liquidize with some water. Place the grain or flour, with enough water to make a thick batter, in bowl uncovered and leave in your kitchen for 2-4 days, depending on the temperature, until it smells sour and bubbles are forming. *But do not let mould form.*
2. Twenty-four hours before you plan to bake the bread, add the remaining ingredients, adjusting the amount of flour to make a fairly soft dough. Turn on to a floured worktop and knead for about 5 minutes.
3. Warm and grease a large bread tin or baking sheet. Shape dough into a loaf, place in or on tin and cover loosely with polythene. Leave at room temperature for 24 hours.
4. Pre-heat oven to 375°F/190°C (Gas Mark 5). Bake bread, which will not have risen much, for 45-50 minutes. Cool on rack. Serve in very thin or medium slices, toasted.

Opposite, clockwise from bottom: Christmas Tree Ginger Biscuits (page 85); Cheese and Sunflower Crackers (page 84); Sesame and Oatmeal Biscuits (page 86); Oatcakes (page 84); Almond Biscuits (page 86).

Croissants

Makes 16.

Very rich in fat, but good for an occasional treat. As they take a long session of cooking, it is a good idea to make two batches, working on one while the other rests, and to freeze them for later use.

Imperial (Metric)

1 lb (450g) malted wholemeal flour or strong plain wholemeal flour
1½ teaspoons micronized yeast
¼ teaspoon vitamin C powder
7 oz (200g) slightly salted butter
11 fl oz (310ml) skim milk, warmed to tepid
Beaten egg to glaze

1. In warmed mixing bowl, blend half the flour with the yeast, vitamin C, salt and milk to make a thick batter. Add remaining flour to form a soft dough.
2. Turn out on to floured worktop, knead for about 8 minutes. Cover with upturned mixing bowl and leave for 30 minutes.
3. Without re-kneading, roll to a rectangle about 9×21-inches (23×52cm). Mark the butter into thirds and dot one third evenly over two-thirds of dough. Fold unbuttered third over, then other end on top. Chill dough for 30 minutes, turn 90 degrees, roll out again and repeat. Repeat with final third of butter. Chill until wanted, covered loosely with polythene.
4. Cut dough in half and roll each piece out in rectangle about 12-inches (30cm) square. Cut into 4 squares, then 8 triangles. Roll each triangle loosely from wide side so that point ends facing down. Place each croissant on baking sheet (ungreased), and cover with polythene.
5. Leave at room temperature until puffy — up to 2 hours. Heat oven to 425°F/220°C (Gas Mark 7). Brush twice with egg, bake for 12-15 minutes. Drain of 'leaked' butter, cool croissants on wire rack.

Variations:
Grated carob or cheese can be thickly sprinkled over the dots of butter.

Croissants

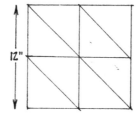 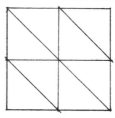

8.
Biscuits

There's a wider choice of biscuits on the market than of almost any other food. You need only look at the shelves of any food shop to be impressed with the national passion for plain, fancy, sweet and savoury biscuits, in dozens of different shapes and sizes.

But if you analyse them, almost all these biscuits are very similar in ingredients — and in having a low food value. Refined flour, a high proportion of hard or artificially hardened fats and an assortment of colourings, flavourings and other additives are what most of them give you — together with a considerable proportion of sugar for the sweet ones. Not to mention the chocolate!

Why not make these simple-recipe items at home, where you can save a surprising amount of money, and end up with something that's tastier and better for you?

Biscuits *are* easy to make. Most of our varieties cook at around the same temperature so it is easy to make more than one kind at once. With the help of a variety of cutters, natural flavours and garnishes, you can turn out a considerable assortment.

Keep in mind these flavourings, which can be added to any plain or sweet biscuit dough: lemon or orange, finely grated rind and juice; decaffeinated coffee granules, crushed; carob powder; vanilla essence (natural is now widely available); almond essence; coconut shreds; cinnamon; ground ginger; chopped toasted nuts; mixed spice; and poppy, sesame or caraway seeds either added to the dough (crush sesame and caraway to let flavour out), or sprinkled on top as a garnish.

One thing your biscuits are unlikely to be is low in fat. It's very difficult to make biscuits crisp without a generous amount of fat. However, you can use better quality fats, such as high pufa margarine, not to mention small amounts of butter (preferably unsalted) for flavour. Each of these recipes has been tested to establish the smallest amount of fat to produce a good result.

Two general tips: don't make your biscuits too thin, as they will tend to become too hard. And time the cooking. Wholemeal flour is already brown so the browning of biscuits is not a good guide. If you overbake them, they will become too hard. Remember, they will crisp up when they cool. If biscuits fail to become crisp, simply re-bake them for 10-15 minutes. The word 'biscuit', in fact, means twice-cooked

The recipes are for medium-sized batches. The exact number will depend on what cutters you use.

Cheese and Sunflower Crackers

Makes 40 1½-inch (4cm) square biscuits. Illustrated opposite page 81.

The Cheddar cheese provides enough fat to moisten these little nibbles.

Imperial (Metric)

4 oz (115g) plain wholemeal flour
¾ teaspoon dry mustard
4 oz (115g) mature Cheddar cheese, finely grated
3 tablespoons plus 1 teaspoon cold water

To garnish:

1 egg white, beaten
A few tablespoons of chopped sunflower seeds

1. Set oven at 450°F/230°C (Gas Mark 8). Lightly grease 2 or 3 baking sheets.
2. Sift mustard with flour. Fork in the cheese, then add water cautiously (since flours vary in their absorption) just until you can form a firm but pliable dough.
3. On a floured worktop, knead only enough to remove cracks, then roll out thinly and cut into shapes. Square biscuits will mean less re-rolling of dough.
4. Place on baking sheets, brush with egg white and garnish with seeds, which should be pressed in lightly. Bake for 10-12 minutes and cool on a rack to crisp.

Oatcakes

Illustrated opposite page 81.

Traditional, Scottish, satisfying with savoury or sweet foods.

Imperial (Metric)

8 oz (225g) medium oatmeal
Large pinch of sea salt (optional)
Pinch of bicarbonate of soda
1 oz (25g) melted butter or hard vegetable fat
Boiling water to mix (about 6 tablespoons)
Wholemeal flour for flouring worktop

1. Set oven to 350°F/180°C (Gas Mark 4).
2. Blend oatmeal, salt (if using) and soda.
3. Add fat to boiling water and, when melted, tip into oatmeal mixture. Form a pliable dough, adding a little more boiling water or oatmeal if needed.
4. Flour worktop and roll mixture out fairly, but not very, thin. Cut into desired shapes, or into circles about 6-inches (15cm) across using a saucer as guide.
5. Place oatcakes on greased baking sheet and if they are large, mark into wedges with a sharp knife.
6. Bake for 25 minutes, removing before they brown. Cool on wire rack.

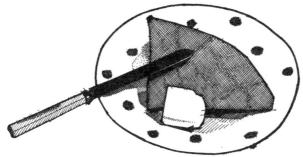

Very Ginger Biscuits

Illustrated opposite page 81.

If you like a really gingery, treacly biscuit, try these.

Imperial (Metric)

4 teaspoons ground ginger
6 oz (170g) plain wholemeal flour
2 oz (55g) high pufa margarine
4 tablespoons black treacle, slightly warmed
1-1½ tablespoons cold water

To glaze:

1 egg white, beaten

1. Set oven to 375°F/190°C (Gas Mark 5).
2. Sieve the ginger and flour, rub in the margarine and fork in the treacle.
3. Add enough water to make dough stick together but not get soft.
4. Roll out about ⅜-inch (0.75cm) thick on floured board and cut biscuits, such as Christmas tree shapes (illustrated opposite page 81). Place on greased baking sheet, brush with egg white and snip with scissors to make decorative top.
5. Bake for 15 minutes.

Almond Biscuits

Illustrated opposite page 81.

These light, semi-sweet biscuits look very professional.

Imperial (Metric)

1 oz (25g) raw cane sugar
2 eggs
1½ tablespoons vegetable oil
Pinch of sea salt
1 oz (25g) ground almonds
5 oz (140g) plain wholemeal flour
1 slightly rounded teaspoon baking powder
About 15 split blanched almonds to garnish

1. Set oven to 375°F/190°C (Gas Mark 5).
2. Grind sugar finely in a coffee mill, food processor or mortar.
3. Transfer to blender goblet or mixing bowl, and beat well with the eggs, oil and salt, reserving a little egg white for glazing.
4. Add the ground almonds. Sift in the flour and baking powder, to make a soft dough.
5. Roll out the mixture just under ¼-inch (5mm) and cut biscuits.
6. Place on lightly greased baking sheet, brush generously with the egg white, place an almond on top and brush again. Bake for 15 minutes or until the biscuits just begin to brown. Cool on rack.

Sesame and Oatmeal Biscuits

Makes about 25. Illustrated opposite page 81.

A basic mixture which can be flavoured to taste in several ways — see introduction to this section for suggestions.

Imperial (Metric)

1 tablespoon sesame seeds
4 oz (115g) plain wholemeal flour
4 oz (115g) fine oatmeal
1 oz (25g) high pufa margarine
1 oz (25g) clear honey, slightly warmed
1 tablespoon skim milk, to mix

1. Set oven to 350°F/180°C (Gas Mark 4).
2. Toast the sesame seeds in ungreased heavy pan over very low heat for 2 minutes, stirring until they begin to jump. Grind in coffee mill or mortar.
3. Mix seeds with the flour and oatmeal, fork in the margarine and honey and form a stiff dough with the milk, if necessary adding a very little cold water.
4. Roll out fairly thin on floured worktop, and cut into desired shapes.
5. Place on greased baking sheet, prick in several places with fork and bake for 15-20 minutes. Cool on rack.

Shortbread

Makes 2 rounds of about 6 pieces each.

You think that the dough will never stick together, but eventually with handling it will, to make a shortbread that's traditional, high-fat, but substantially less greasy than most.

Imperial (Metric)

4 oz (115g) butter or *a mixture of butter and high pufa margarine*
2 oz (55g) Demerara sugar
7 oz (200g) plain wholemeal flour
1 oz (25g) ground brown rice (from health food stores)
2 tablespoons water

1. Set oven to 325°F/160°C (Gas Mark 3).
2. Cream the fat and sugar thoroughly.
3. Add the flour, rice flour and water. The mixture will seem very crumbly, but after kneading will eventually form a ball which can be rolled out, albeit with a few cracks.
4. Divide the mixture in two, and roll out on greased baking sheet into circles about ⅜-inch (1cm) thick. Smooth out cracks with your fingers.
5. With two fingers, pinch up edge of each circle decoratively, then prick the shortbread all the way through, covering the surface evenly, using a sharp-pronged fork. If liked, mark into segments with a sharp knife.
6. Bake for about 40 minutes, cool on wire rack.

Peanut Rusks

Rugged, but with a certain chewy appeal.

Imperial (Metric)

6 oz (170g) crunchy peanut butter
8 oz (225g) plain wholemeal flour
2 teaspoons yeast extract
¼ pint (140ml) skim milk
1 egg

1. Set oven to 350°F/180°C (Gas Mark 4).
2. Fork peanut butter and flour together. Liquidize the yeast extract, milk and egg and pour into flour mixture, forming a pliable dough.
3. Transfer to a greased small, deep-ish baking tin about 1-inch (2.5cm) deep. Bake for 45 minutes.
4. Remove from oven, cut into fingers. Now remove these from tin, and cut each horizontally into two. Place on baking sheet and return to oven.
5. Bake for a further 20-30 minutes, then cool to crisp on rack. If the rusks are not crisp enough, re-bake (later if more convenient) for 10-15 minutes at the same temperature.

Garibaldi Biscuits

Imperial (Metric)

1 batch shortcrust wholemeal pastry (page 25) or scone dough (page 21)

Filling:

6 oz (170g) currants, well washed
1 teaspoon mixed spice

1. Heat oven to 375°F/190°C (Gas Mark 4).
2. Roll out shortcrust pastry thinly, into an oblong.
3. Sprinkle half the pastry with currants and spice.
4. Fold over other half, run rolling pin over the 'sandwich' pressing the two layers and currants firmly together. Mark deeply with knife into fingers.
5. Bake for 20 minutes. Cut or break into fingers while still warm. Cool on rack.

Wheat Crisps

Makes 10.

Could also be described as a crisp chapatti. This recipe really needs a very heavy based, e.g., cast iron, pan or griddle. The result is something like a round crispbread or matzo.

Imperial (Metric)

8 oz (225g) plain wholemeal flour
Large pinch of sea salt (optional)
About 6 fl oz (170ml) water
A little vegetable oil for cooking

1. Mix flour and salt, add the water to make a pliable dough.
2. Knead on a floured worktop for 3-4 minutes.
3. Divide into 10 pieces, roll each ball into as thin a circle as possible. You'll find you can stretch the dough gently with your hands without it breaking.
4. Heat a heavy-based skillet or griddle, preferably cast iron. Brush very lightly with oil. Heat the grill.
5. Place first circle of dough on pan and cook for about 30 seconds on each side.
6. Place this round under grill for about 30 seconds, while you put the second round on to cook — and so on.
7. If you want crisp rounds, cool on wire rack. For soft, chappati-style rounds, cover with lid while cooking and place in folds of a teacloth after cooking to prevent steam escaping.

9.
Special Occasions

A highlight of special occasions is the food. It's tempting to stick to tried-and-tested recipes, especially for expensive items like rich fruit cakes. Many of us also hesitate to try new ways in case our conservative family or friends look askance.

The recipes in this section can easily become the new 'traditional' recipes in your household. They are reliable, traditional in character and far superior to bought versions. Why should we stick to recipes that we think of as traditional, but are really only a product of the last century, when versions that are in a way *more* traditional — using ingredients from before the age of refining, and also better for us — produce just as delicious results?

Christmas Tree Bread

Illustrated opposite page 97.

A pretty centrepiece for a Christmas table. You can also make teddybears (children can be very bloodthirsty!) for birthday parties.

Imperial (Metric)

Rich dough, as for Fruit Ring (page 63) or *regular bread dough, if preferred (page 74)*
Beaten egg to glaze

1. Knead mixed dough for 5-8 minutes.
2. Warm and grease a large baking sheet. Divide the dough into 17 equal pieces. Roll each into a ball.
3. Arrange on baking sheet as illustrated, setting balls not quite touching so they will join but keep their shape on rising.
4. Cover with unprinted polythene and leave at room temperature for about 40 minutes. Heat oven to maximum.
5. Brush loaf with egg, then with kitchen scissors, make small snips in top of each sphere to give an effect as in the picture (opposite page 97).

6. Bake for 10 minutes, then reduce heat to 425°F/220°C (Gas Mark 7) for further 15 minutes, or until bread is golden.
7. Remove from oven and allow to cool slightly before transferring carefully to wire rack. To serve, tie a satin ribbon around the 'trunk'.

Very Rich Plumcake

Makes a deep 7-inch (18cm) diameter cake. Illustrated between pages 64 and 65.

Suitable for all the 'rich fruit cake' occasions, such as Christmas, Easter, weddings or birthdays. Ring the changes by exchanging the prunes for dates if wished, or using different nuts or alcohol.

Imperial (Metric)

2 oz (55g) dried apricots, washed and soaked
4 oz (115g) prunes, stoned
¼ pint (140ml) water
3 oz (85g) high pufa margarine or butter, or a mixture
3 eggs, beaten
8 oz (225g) plain wholemeal flour
2 teaspoons baking powder
1½ teaspoons mixed spice
2 oz (55g) almonds, chopped and toasted
1 lb 6 oz (625g) mixed dried fruit, washed
Juice and finely grated rind of ½ orange
2 tablespoons brandy, whisky or rum

1. Simmer apricots and prunes in the water for 15 minutes. Check all stones have been removed from prunes and liquidize mixture in blender.
2. Pour into very large mixing bowl. Add all the other ingredients, beating in the eggs one at a time very thoroughly. The mixture should be a dropping consistency.
3. Set oven to 325°F/160°C (Gas Mark 3). Grease and line a 7-inch (18cm) cake tin, greasing the inside of lining paper as well. Spoon mixture into tin, making a depression in centre to discourage the cake forming a peak.
4. Bake for 30 minutes, then reduce heat to 300°F/150°C (Gas Mark 3) and bake for another hour. Cover top loosely with foil if it over-browns.
5. Test with skewer which will come out dry if cake is cooked. Cool for a few minutes in tin before turning on to wire rack. Stores well in airtight tin.

Christmas Pudding

Makes three medium or four 1 lb (450g) puddings.

If you are worried about trying a new recipe, make a batch and enjoy one before Christmas comes.

Imperial (Metric)

1½ lb (680g) mixed dried fruit, washed, chopped where necessary and dried
10 oz (285g) wholemeal breadcrumbs
6 oz (170g) mixed peel, chopped
8 oz (225g) high pufa margarine
3 oz (85g) almonds, chopped
3 oz (85g) grated carrot
4 oz (115g) plain wholemeal flour
1 teaspoon baking powder
2 teaspoons mixed spice
¼ teaspoon grated nutmeg
2 tablespoons molasses
4 eggs
Rind of 1 lemon, finely grated
Juice of 1 lemon
5 fl oz (140ml) brandy or rum
Skim milk, ale or water, to mix

1. In a clean washing up bowl, combine 1 lb (450g) of the dried fruit with the breadcrumbs, peel, margarine, almonds and carrot.
2. Sift the flour with the baking powder, spice and nutmeg and add to the bowl.
3. In the liquidizer, blend the remaining dried fruit with the molasses, eggs, lemon rind, lemon juice and brandy or rum. Stir into the main mixture. Add liquid to make a soft, dropping consistency.
4. Turn the mixture into well-greased pudding basins, allowing room to rise. Cover with foil, making a pleat in the centre to allow for expansion. Tie with non-synthetic string.
5. Boil some water. Place each basin in a saucepan large enough to be tightly covered over the top of basin. Pour in boiling water to reach about two-thirds up side of basins. Bring water to the boil again.
6. Cover tightly and simmer, topping up water as necessary from time to time. Steam small puddings for 5 hours, larger ones for 7½-8 hours, then for about 2 and 3 hours respectively before serving.

Variation:
For a lower fat pudding, use only 6 oz (170g) margarine.

Storage.
The safest way to store this type of lower-fat, lower-sugar pudding is by freezing it. To achieve this, cook in one of the plastic pudding basins often sold with lids.

Mock Marzipan

Makes a thin layer for a 7-inch (18cm) cake.

Adapted from a wartime recipe, from a leaflet on Christmas baking by Harrods, the 'top people's store'. Why revive it? Because it's rather good. It's also suitable for those who want a lower fat topping than almond paste.

Imperial (Metric)

1 oz (25g) high pufa margarine or butter or mixture
1 tablespoon water
2-3 teaspoons honey, to taste
2 oz (55g) soya flour or 2½ oz (70g) wholemeal semolina (from health food stores) or a
* mixture of half the given quantity of each*
1 scant teaspoon natural almond flavouring

1. Heat the fat, water, honey and half the almond essence. (Brands of almond flavouring vary in strength so it is wisest to adjust this at the end.)
2. When melted, remove from heat and stir in the semolina, though soya flour should be sieved first as it tends to get lumpy in storage. Adjust honey and flavouring.
3. Knead briefly to smooth, roll out between two sheets of polythene as it becomes more fragile when cold.
4. Peel off top polythene layer, invert topping over cake and peel off other polythene layer. Trim edges and use pieces to make tiny balls as part of cake decoration.

Almond Paste

Covers a 7-inch (18cm) cake.

A simple and pleasantly soft covering for rich fruit cakes. You can then press in decorative nuts or dried fruit, or other decorations.

Imperial (Metric)

1 egg white
4 tablespoons honey, warmed
2-3 teaspoons lemon juice
A few drops of almond essence
4 oz (115g) ground almonds
2 teaspoons soya flour
2 tablespoon jam, preferably apricot

1. Beat egg white to soft peaks, continuing beating as you then pour the honey into the mixture little by little. Beat in the lemon juice and almond essence.
2. Stir in the almonds and soya flour. You should have a pliable paste. If it is too soft, stir in a little more soya flour. Brush cake with jam.
3. Roll out between two sheets of unprinted polythene to the size of cake. Remove top sheet, invert paste and bottom sheet over cake and peel off polythene. Trim edges neatly and use trimmings to make decorations.

Decorations:
You can sandwich two halves of dried apricots, well washed, with a small ball of the almond paste, and then stick half an almond in each ball. Or blanched almond or walnut halves can be sandwiched with small balls of paste.

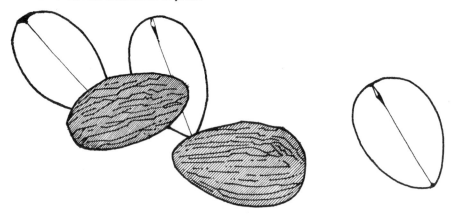

Mince Pies

Making mince pies is, for me, an important part of the Christmas feeling.

Imperial (Metric)

Mincemeat:

4 oz (115g) each sultanas, raisins and currants, washed
2 oz (55g) dried apricots
2 medium eating apples, peeled
Juice of 1 orange and 1 lemon
Finely grated rind of 1 lemon
2 teaspoons mixed spice
2 teaspoons cinnamon
1 oz (25g) almonds, chopped
2-3 tablespoons brandy
Honey to taste, about 1 tablespoon

For the pies:

12 oz (350g) plain wholemeal flour
6 oz (170g) high pufa margarine, or mixture with butter
Beaten egg to glaze
A little raw cane sugar, for decoration

1. In mincer or food processor, mince finely all the dried fruit and the apples. Mix with all the remaining mincemeat ingredients.
2. Taste, and add extra honey as wanted.
3. Pot the mixture in freezer container. Refrigerate for 3-4 days to allow fruit to swell and flavours to develop before freezing.
4. Make the pastry by rubbing fat into flour, then adding enough very cold water to bind mixture into a very dry dough.
5. Roll out on floured worktop and cut discs to fit the base of deep patty tins.
6. Line patty tins, fill with mincemeat and cut smaller pastry discs for top.
7. Set oven to 375°F/190°C (Gas Mark 5). Brush the tops with the egg, sprinkle with a few grains of sugar, and make two slits for steam to escape.
8. Bake for 15 minutes.

Hot Cross Buns

Illustrated opposite.

Bought hot cross buns seem miserably short of currants and flavour, and don't create the mood of the season as these can.

Imperial (Metric)

1 lb (450g) plain wholemeal flour
1½ teaspoons micronized yeast
¼ teaspoon vitamin C powder
2 teaspoons mixed spice
1 teaspoon cinnamon
6 oz (170g) currants, washed
2 oz (55g) chopped orange or lemon rind
1 egg (or 2 if preferred), reserving a little for glazing
2 tablespoons honey
2 oz (55g) high pufa margarine or butter or mixture
½ pint (285ml) skim milk, warmed (110°F/43°C)

For the crosses:

1 oz (25g) ground almonds
A few drops of almond essence
2 oz (55g) plain wholemeal flour
Water to mix

1. Mix all bun ingredients together, increasing the amount of milk a little if necessary, to make a soft dough.
2. Knead on floured worktop for 5-8 minutes. Cover with upturned mixing bowl while you make crosses mixture.
3. Mix almonds, essence, flour and just enough water to make a dough. Roll out and cut into thin strips.
4. Cut bun dough into pieces to make buns about two-thirds of desired final size. Shape. Place on warmed, greased baking sheet.
5. Cover buns with sheet of unprinted polythene and leave for about 45 minutes to rise. Use almond mixture strips to make crosses.
6. Heat oven to maximum temperature. Brush buns, if wished, with reserved egg. Bake for 5 minutes, then reduce heat to 425°F/220°C (Gas Mark 7) for further 10 minutes. If wished, brush with a mixture of honey and water when removing from oven to produce softer-topped buns.

Opposite: Yeast Fruit Cake (page 62) *and* Hot Cross Buns (above).

Nut Nibbles

Makes about 20.

Make these very small for the best effect. Serve on a plate of greenery.

Imperial (Metric)

4 oz (115g) nuts, freshly ground
2 oz (55g) wholemeal breadcrumbs
1 teaspoon yeast extract
About 6 tablespoons boiling water to mix

1. Toast all the nuts in ungreased pan over a low heat, stirring, for 4 minutes or until they start to smell nice.
2. Mix three-quarters of them with the breadcrumbs.
3. Dissolve the yeast extract in the water and use to moisten the mixture. Add a little more water if required to bind.
4. Place remaining nuts in deep bowl. Use fingers to form small balls of nut and crumb mixture, place one at a time in bowl of nuts and swirl bowl to coat balls with nuts. Chill before serving with sticks of carrot and celery.

Opposite: Coffee and Apricot Gateau (page 98) *and* Christmas Tree Bread (page 90).

Coffee and Apricot Gateau

Illustrated opposite page 97.

A very unusual moist, cheesecake-like gateau.

Imperial (Metric)

6 oz (170g) dried apricots, washed
6 fl oz (170ml) skim milk
3 oz (85g) high pufa margarine
2 eggs
6 oz (170g) plain wholemeal flour
2 teaspoons instant decaffeinated coffee (if using granules, crush)
½ teaspoon bicarbonate of soda
1 teaspoon cream of tartar
Orange juice to make a dropping consistency, about 1 tablespoon

Garnish:

3 oz (85g) dried apricot halves, washed

Filling:

12 oz (350g) low fat smooth soft cheese
1 teaspoon instant decaffeinated coffee (if using granules, crush)
2 tablespoons clear honey
Coffee or orange liqueur to flavour, about 1 tablespoon

1. Place apricots for cake and apricots for garnish in separate small saucepans. Cover with water, boil, drain. Cover with fresh water, and bring to the boil again. Cover and simmer both pans for 20 minutes.
2. Drain apricots for garnish and set aside. Return cake apricots to pan, cover with the milk and boil again, stirring over moderate heat as skim milk burns easily.
3. Remove pan from heat, and liquidize. Add the margarine and eggs, blending until smooth.
4. Set oven to 350°F/180°C (Gas Mark 4).
5. Sieve the flour, coffee and raising agents, retaining any bran left in the sieve. Combine the wet and dry mixtures, adding enough orange juice to make a consistency where the mixture will drop from a spoon.
6. Grease well two 7-inch (18cm) sandwich tins. Flour with the reserved bran. Divide mixture between tins, making a slight dip in centre of mixture. Bake for about 25 minutes, until just firm in centre. Leave in tins for one or two minutes, then cool on a rack.
7. Blend filling ingredients thoroughly. When cakes are cool, halve each one horizontally (they will be moist inside) and sandwich to make a single cake with filling layers.

8. Reserve a little filling to spread over cake top. Arrange apricot halves over this. If liked, glaze with a little warmed apricot jam or warmed honey.

Variation:
Substitute 1-2 tablespoons sieved carob powder, to taste, for coffee in filling.

Cheese Flakes

Makes about 40.

Delicious little mouthfuls which go down well at parties.

Imperial (Metric)

½ mix yeast pastry (page 26)

Filling:

5 oz (140g) reduced fat Cheddar cheese, finely grated
1 teaspoon oil
4 oz (115g) mushrooms, washed, unpeeled and chopped fairly finely
1 large egg, beaten
¼ teaspoon cayenne pepper
Pinch of sea salt (optional)
2-3 tablespoons chopped chives, spring onions or parsley

1. Set oven to 425°F/220°C (Gas Mark 7).
2. Sauté mushrooms in pan brushed with the oil for 8 minutes.
3. Mix cheese, mushrooms, egg, cayenne pepper, salt if using, and chopped herbs.
4. Roll out yeast pastry very thinly and cut out small circles of dough using a wine glass.
5. Using egg reserved from making yeast pastry, brush edge of each circle with egg, place a large teaspoonful of filling on one half and fold other half over to make a semi-circle. Press edges to seal and place on greased baking sheet.
6. Repeat. Brush with remaining egg and bake for 15 minutes. Serve hot.

10.
Crumbs

Don't waste stale bread: there are many ways to turn it into a useful ingredient.

Use stale bread to make **breadcrumbs**, either in a blender or food processor for soft crumbs, or by toasting on an ungreased baking sheet in the oven at around 350°F/180°C (Gas Mark 4) for about 30 minutes or until crisp. Place in a polythene bag and crush into crumbs with rolling pin. Store in an airtight jar for 4-5 days or freeze. Use for stuffings, to thicken sauces, soups and casseroles and for puddings, if making fresh crumbs. Use dried crumbs for coating or topping purposes.

Make **croûtons** for serving with soups or savoury dishes. Either spread stale bread with margarine or butter, cut into cubes and toast on baking sheet under grill; or fry in the minimum of oil.

For **bread sauce**, heat ½ pint (285ml) skim milk slowly with a halved onion, 1 clove and a bay leaf. Stir as skim milk burns more easily. Remove from heat, then remove clove and bayleaf. Either remove onion or liquidize with the milk plus 2 oz (55g) fresh wholemeal breadcrumbs, ½ oz (15g) butter or high pufa margarine and seasoning to taste. Heat slowly until thick.

Left over sandwiches can be toasted, or spread on the outside with high pufa margarine or butter, mixed with yeast extract if liked, then grilled for a minute or two on each side.

Cream Cheese Dumplings: soak pieces of bread in skim milk, squeeze out excess. Mash with smooth low fat soft cheese, a little honey, a little grated lemon rind and 1 egg per 4 oz (115g) mixture. Drop balls of mixture formed with 2 tablespoons into gently simmering water and cook for 10 minutes. Serve with fruit dishes.

Veiled Peasant Girl: Poach slices of apple in a little apple juice until just tender. Fry wholemeal breadcrumbs in a skillet lightly brushed with high pufa margarine or butter. Remove from heat, stir in a spoonful of honey or raw cane sugar, plus a pinch of ground cloves or cinnamon. Layer apples and crumbs in individual dishes and serve chilled with egg custard, plain yogurt or cream.

Barbecue Bread: cut stale bread into thick slices. Spread with a mixture of equal parts of high pufa margarine and mature Cheddar cheese, grated, mashed with a few drops Worcestershire sauce, a little mustard powder and chopped spring onions. Reform slices into loaf, wrap in foil and bake in a hot oven for 15 minutes.

Bread Stuffing (for poultry or vegetables): mix 3 cups of wholemeal breadcrumbs with 1 sautéd, finely chopped onion, ½ teaspoon powdered dried thyme, 2 oz (55g) high pufa margarine, sea salt and pepper.

French Toast: for each person, beat in a large flat dish 1 egg with a half-eggshell-amount of skim milk, a large pinch of sea salt (optional) and a dab of honey. Soak 2 slices of wholemeal bread in the mixture for a few minutes, turning.

Brush a skillet with oil, heat thoroughly and brown slices for about 1 minute on each side. Serve immediately. This makes a good breakfast, quick snack or accompaniment to stewed fruit.

Melba Toast: toast thick slices of stale bread on both sides. Remove crusts, lay each slice on its side and carefully cut through soft centre to make two thin slices. This is easy to do when the toast is warm.

Either grill, untoasted side up, on medium heat, or bake in hot oven. In either case, be careful the toast does not burn. It will curl, so place several inches from grill flame. Keep in airtight tin to serve with soup, pâté, cheese, etc.

Brown Betty: fill a baking dish with chopped fresh fruit, then cover with 4 oz (115g) wholemeal breadcrumbs. Mix 3 tablespoons honey with 2 tablespoons orange juice and ½ teaspoon ground ginger, and pour over the crumbs. Bake 325°F/170°C (Gas Mark 3) for about 40 minutes, or until fruit is tender. This dish can be made with finely chopped apples, pears, plums, soft fruit, rhubarb or any mixture. The amount of honey needed will depend on the sweetness of the fruit used. If uncertain about this, stew fruit in a very little water first, and sweeten to taste. Then halve honey in mixture poured over.

Spanish Pudding: sauté 1 onion and 1 green pepper, both chopped, in 2 teaspoons of oil in thick-based pan with lid on for 10 minutes. Mash 4 oz (115g) wholemeal bread with a small can of tomatoes, add to onion and pepper with 1 tablespoon chopped parsley, 1 egg, 4 oz (115g) grated mature or reduced fat Cheddar cheese, and a dash of Worcestershire sauce. Add a little skim milk if necessary to give a soft consistency. Transfer to small greased oven dish and bake at 350°F/180°C (Gas Mark 4) for 30 minutes.

Mushroom Bake: brush a thick-based pan with oil, heat and add 8 oz (225g) sliced but unpeeled mushrooms. Cook over low heat for 8 minutes. Meanwhile, mix 6 oz (170g) wholemeal breadcrumbs with a small, finely chopped onion, 6 oz (170g) mature or reduced fat Cheddar cheese, grated, 2 oz (55g) high pufa margarine and seasoning.

Press half the mixture into a lightly greased oven dish, top with the mushrooms and finish with remaining mixture. Sprinkle a little more grated cheese on top. Bake at 375°F/190°C (Gas Mark 5) for about 30 minutes.

Mrs Beeton's Bread Soup: break 4 oz (115g) stale wholemeal bread into small pieces, place in a large saucepan and cover with 1¾ pints (1 litre) well-flavoured stock. If you don't have suitable stock, make it up with *Vecon* vegetable concentrate. Leave until soft, mash with a fork, then simmer for 10 minutes, check seasoning and serve sprinkled with chopped parsley.

Cheese Chops

Serves 4. Illustrated opposite page 112.

Very simple — very nice.

Imperial (Metric)

4 oz (115g) mature or reduced fat Cheddar cheese, grated
4 oz (115g) wholemeal breadcrumbs, half soft, half dried
2 eggs, beaten
1 teaspoon dry mustard
A large pinch of freshly ground black pepper
2 tablespoons chopped parsley

1. Mix the cheese with the soft breadcrumbs, eggs, mustard, pepper and parsley. Reserve a small amount of egg for coating.
2. Divide the mixture into four and shape into 'chops'. Egg and breadcrumb, then grill on a greased baking sheet for a few minutes at high heat on each side.

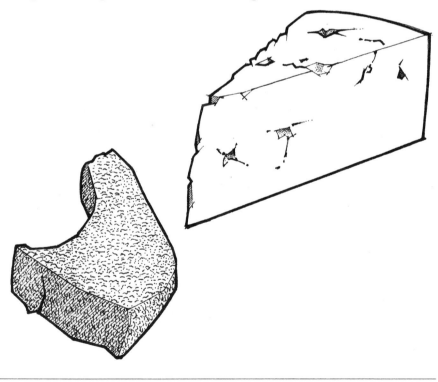

Stuffed Courgettes

Serves 4. Illustrated opposite page 112.

The lemon juice brings out the flavour here.

Imperial (Metric)

4 large courgettes
4 oz (115g) wholemeal breadcrumbs
8 oz (225g) cottage or curd cheese
Finely grated rind and juice of 1 lemon
4 tablespoons flaked almonds
Paprika to garnish

1. Boil a very large saucepan half full of water.
2. Set oven to 375°F/190°C (Gas Mark 5).
3. Plunge courgettes into boiling water for 6 minutes. Halve lengthways and scoop out centres. Place 'boats' in greased shallow casserole or roasting dish.
4. Mash scooped out flesh with breadcrumbs, cheese, lemon juice and two-thirds of the almonds. Pile mixture along courgette centres.
5. Cover dish, bake for 30 minutes. Remove lid, sprinkle with reserved almonds and paprika and bake for a further 15 minutes uncovered.

11.
High Fibre

Wholemeal flour naturally contains plenty of fibre, so why take extra? The answer is simple for many people who've been used to taking laxatives for years: they find that wheat bran, say a tablespoonful per day, keeps their digestive system working without artificial and irritant medicines.

But while a little bran can be helpful, more is not 'better'. It's much healthier to eat your fibre in the foods in which it naturally occurs than to take spoonfuls of wheat bran on top of refined food.

In food, fibre goes with natural, unprocessed ingredients. By eating more of these, you get the benefit of their extra vitamins and minerals as well as of fibre. As carbohydrate stops being a 'dirty' word, with nutritionists recommending we eat more of our food in this form than as high-fat or high-sugar dishes, the contribution of vitamins and minerals we expect to get from carbohydrate is rising. If we switch from meat to white bread, we still get protein, but we lose a considerable amount of vitamins and minerals.

The other reason not to adopt the 'bran with everything' approach is that, while bran contains significant amounts of zinc, calcium and iron, it also contains phytic acid which can combine with these minerals, forming compounds from which the body cannot extract the mineral.

In the process of fermentation, whether in bread or cake-making, much of this phytic acid is broken down, so you get more minerals out of your food. Eating ounces of raw bran a day, in contrast, could reduce your mineral supply. If you eat a refined food diet, you won't have many minerals to spare. Particularly when people start eating extra wheat bran, their system may not be used to conserving minerals; regular wholewheat eaters are thought to adjust so they keep in mineral balance in spite of more phytic acid.

High Fibre Foods

Fibre is a 'family' name for a range of complex carbohydrates which are not fully digested by the body, but which travel through the body providing valuable bulk and padding for food wastes. The effect is a smoother-working digestive system.

However, research is showing that it's worth getting your fibre from different foods, because different types behave differently inside you.

While large particles of wheat bran, for instance, are considered the form of fibre that most speeds the passage of food through the intestinal system — the so-called 'transit time' — the kind of 'gummy' fibre found in foods like oats and pulses seems to have a different useful effect.

These 'soluble' fibres have been shown to slow down the absorption of calories from food, releasing a slower, longer-lasting flow into the bloodstream. As food stays longer in your stomach, you may feel fuller for longer — very useful for slimmers. And the lower rise in the level of glucose in the bloodstream (the body makes blood sugar from all foods, not just from sugar itself), can be useful to the many people whose bodies react badly to a dramatic surge in sugar. Such a surge is a modern phenomenon since, in the past, most food was of the slowly-absorbed kind. The sugar in the bloodstream stimulates the production of insulin, necessary for its transformation into useable energy. A sudden surge of sugar may over-strain the body's insulin production mechanism in vulnerable people causing dramatic see-sawing of the body's blood-sugar levels.

Eating more oats and pulses is now recommended to provide this type of fibre. There's also some evidence that doing so can reduce the level of cholesterol in the bloodstream. While the cholesterol eaten in food is no longer considered the 'bogey man' behind all heart disease, as the body makes cholesterol itself and other events can raise blood cholesterol levels (such as smoking or stress), a high level is definitely considered a danger signal.

Some people inherit a tendency to a high level, and they need medical detection and treatment. But for most of us, the rise in cholesterol takes place fairly slowly after years of the kinds of living habits that favour it: smoking, overweight, lack of exercise and simply eating too much. Too much stress can push it up too. Taking extra wheat bran has not been shown to reduce the level; hence the growing enthusiasm for other forms of fibre. You can now buy oatbran and soya bran in health food stores. These can be added to food in much the same way as wheatbran.

Other kinds of fibre are found in fruit and vegetables, with the most obvious benefit of providing filling, colourful foods which are generally low in calories.

Include all three kinds — wheat fibre, oat/pulse fibre, and fruit/vegetable fibre — in your meals, just by eating plenty of these foods. Here is an example of a day's high fibre eating, without added bran, compared to a low-fibre day which is typical of many people's meals.

Your Daily Fibre

Examples of how an average day's food could provide well below 30 grams — the recommended amount — or by using wholemeal, effortlessly enough.

Meals	Low Fibre	grams of dietary fibre	High Fibre	grams of dietary fibre
Breakfast:	2 slices white toast (total weight 70g)	1.9	2 slices of wholemeal toast (total weight 70g)	6
	1 apple (5 oz/140g)	2.8		
	Spread on bread	—	1 apple (5 oz/140g)	2.8
	Milk in drink	—	Spread on bread	—
	Honey on bread	—	Milk in drink	—
			Honey on bread	—

Meals	Low Fibre	grams of dietary fibre	High Fibre	grams of dietary fibre
Break:	1 custard cream biscuit (⅓ oz/10g)	.4	1 oatcake biscuit (⅓ oz/10g)	1.3
Lunch:	Sausages and mash	1	Wholemeal pizza	5
	Peas (85g)	4.4	Bean salad (85g)	6.3
	Green salad (85g)	1.3	Green salad (85g)	1.3
	Fruit yogurt	negligible	Banana (100g peeled)	3.4
Break:	White bun (40g)	.9	Wholemeal bun (40g)	3.4
Dinner:	Chicken casserole	negligible	Chicken casserole	negligible
	White rice (55g raw)	1.3	Brown rice (55g) raw)	2.6
	Rhubarb fool	2.6	Rhubarb wholemeal crumble	5
		16.6		37.1

Adding ¼ oz (7g) bran to this meal pattern (as much as is palatable on breakfast cereal) will only add 3.1 grams of fibre.

This style of eating provides some bean, fruit and oat fibre as well as wheat and rice fibre.

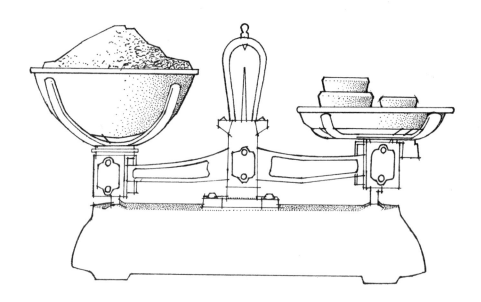

High Fibre Recipes for Those who Feel They Want a Little More

You can alternate wheat, oat or soya bran in the biscuits or muffins.

Oat Bran Biscuits

Illustrated opposite page 113.

A basic biscuit that goes well with savoury or sweet foods.

Imperial (Metric)

3 oz (85g) plain wholemeal flour
2 oz (55g) high pufa margarine
2 oz (55g) oatbran
Pinch of sea salt (optional)

1. Set oven to 400°F/200°C (Gas Mark 6).
2. Rub fat into flour, stir in oatbran and salt.
3. Add a very little cold water to form a firm dough.
4. Roll out thinly and cut into any desired shape.
5. Bake on greased sheet for 10-15 minutes until just beginning to change colour. Cool on wire rack.

Variations:
Add ½ teaspoon of crushed caraway, fennel or coriander seeds to the mixture before adding water.

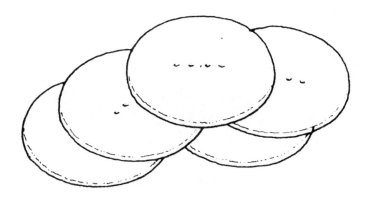

Rough Bread

Makes 2 small or 1 very large loaf. Illustrated opposite page 113.

For people who like bread with personality. Having made this, the variations you can dream up with different grains and seeds will be many and fun.

Imperial (Metric)

1 lb (450g) favourite wholemeal flour
2 oz (55g) rolled oats
1 oz (25g) wheat germ
4 oz (115g) cooked brown rice or other whole grain
1 oz (25g) sesame seeds, toasted and crushed
2 teaspoons micronized yeast
1 teaspoon molasses
1 tablepoon butter or high pufa margarine
½ teaspoon sea salt
1 egg
½ pint (285ml) lukewarm water
¼ teaspoon vitamin C powder

1. In large bowl, mix all the ingredients.
2. Turn on to floured worktop and knead for about 7 minutes. Cover with upturned bowl and leave for 15-20 minutes.
3. Re-knead briefly, then shape into 2 loaves.
4. Warm and grease 2 small loaf tins or 1 large one. Place bread in tins, cover with polythene and leave to rise for about 1 hour or until doubled in bulk.
5. Heat oven to its highest temperature.
6. Bake bread for 10 minutes, then reduce heat to 400°F/200°C (Gas Mark 6) for further 30 minutes. Cool on wire rack.

Variations:
This bread can be varied in many ways, using different flours — from finest to coarsest grist; different seeds — such as poppy or linseed; and different grains.

American-Style Bran Muffins

Makes about 10. Illustrated opposite page 113.

Lighter than the average muffin.

Imperial (Metric)

4 oz (115g) plain wholemeal flour
¾ teaspoon bicarbonate of soda
Pinch of sea salt (optional)
½ oz (15g) wheat or oat bran
8 fl oz (225ml) buttermilk or skim milk soured by heating gently over a low heat for 2-3
  minutes with a squeeze of lemon juice
1 oz (25g) sultanas
1 tablespoon honey
1 tablespoon molasses or black treacle
¾ oz (20g) high pufa margarine

1. Set oven to 425°F/220°C (Gas Mark 7).
2. Sift flour, soda and salt. Stir in bran.
3. Heat the milk with the sultanas, molasses/treacle, honey and margarine just to soften
   these ingredients.
4. Add these to flour mixture and beat for 40 strokes.
5. Pour into paper cases or greased deep bun tin.
6. Bake for 15-20 minutes until just firm.

Variations:
Blueberries, chopped apple and spice are all traditional additions to muffins. As any kind of
fruit tends to sink to the bottom of the muffin, the best way to add it is to fill cases only ⅔
full and sprinkle fruit in just before baking. Use sweet fruit, or double amount of honey in
the recipe.

12.
Food to Take with You

With an increasing number of children taking a packed lunch to school, more of us taking lunch to work and the popularity of picnics, many of us eat something like a third of our meals away from home.

Wholemeal cooking can make these occasions more enjoyable, a treat of a meal instead of a stopgap until we get home. Nutritionally, packed cold meals can be just as good for you as what is termed a 'proper' cooked meal. Developing a range of packed meals that your family like, and which are convenient to prepare, can take the burden out of making packed meals, and remove the temptation to fill the lunchbox with high-fat foods like crisps, chocolate or tooth-rotting sweets.

Sandwiches

Made with wholemeal flour and a lower-fat filling, sandwiches are as satisfying and nutritious as a cooked main course. The bread will stay moist, and there is less need to get the filling right to the edges: wholemeal bread has more flavour of its own. If you want more variety in sandwiches, change the shape or type of bread you use, as well as the fillings.

Spreads

As well as high pufa margarine or softened butter, try these spreads:

- half-and-half mix of high pufa margarine and butter
- mix of half high pufa margarine and half low-fat soft cheese, sieved if smooth type is not available.
- flavour your high pufa margarine with yeast extract, chopped parsley or freshly ground black pepper.

Fillings

Higher-fat fillings, such as peanut butter, hard or cream cheese, pâté, sausages, bacon, sandwich spread or egg mayonnaise won't hurt if eaten occasionally.

But for every day, stress the lower fat choices, such as:

- yeast extract (now available in low salt form from health food stores), combined with salad and/or cottage cheese.

- cottage cheese combined with mashed smoked fish, hard-boiled egg, chopped olives, grated carrot, freshly chopped herbs (mint is surprisingly nice like this), chopped apples tossed with lemon or orange juice, mashed banana, mashed cooked dried apricots, mustard and cress, chopped cucumber or watercress.
- plain salad, and have more rounds of sandwiches.
- lean chicken, turkey or mashed chicken livers, all with salad.
- mashed tuna, sardines or other tinned fish, all well drained to minimize fat and salt content.

One way of making sandwiches more convenient is to make a large batch *without* salad filling, and freeze. The required amount can be taken out each day and placed in a lunchbox where it will thaw in 3-4 hours in time for lunch.

Hard-boiled egg and salad do not freeze well. Add chunks of carrot, celery, cucumber or other raw vegetables to the lunchbox separately.

Alternatives to Sandwiches

- rolls packed with the filling and salad separate.
- plain Scones (page 21) cut with wide cutter, split and filled as sandwiches.

Other Savouries

- slices of Pizza (page 30), Savoury Bread Pudding (page 43), Leek Pasties (page 112), Savoury Raised Pie (page 40), Quiche (page 37), Cheese Baps (page 78), Falafel (page 36), Celery and Walnut Savoury (page 29), Savoury Tea Loaf (page 113), or Cheese Chops (page 102).

In every case, include something fresh, from a peeled carrot to sticks of cucumber, in the lunchbox.

Filling Up the Corners

- soup, chilled or hot, in a vacuum flask
- fresh fruit, with small knife for peeling
- a handful of dried fruit, well washed
- buns, cakes or fruit loaf from cake section (page 60)
- sweet scones (page 21)
- biscuits, from biscuit section (page 83)
- hard-boiled egg — for occasional use
- yogurt in small jar, mixed with mashed dried fruit or chopped fresh fruit avoiding those which discolour, i.e., apples and pears
- baked apples stuffed with dried fruit and sprinkled with cinnamon, cold.

Leek Pasties

Makes about 6. Illustrated inside front cover.

An ideal food for travelling, these are extremely tasty.

Imperial (Metric)

6 oz (170g) plain wholemeal flour
1 teaspoon micronized yeast
1 large egg, beaten
3 fl oz (85ml) skim milk, just warmer than your finger (110°F/43°C)
1 oz (25g) high pufa margarine
Pinch of sea salt (optional)

Filling:

1 teaspoon vegetable oil
3 tablepoons water
½ teaspoon Vecon
4 oz (115g) carrots, finely diced
8 oz (225g) leeks, green and white, finely chopped
2 tablespoons rolled oats
8 oz (225g) cottage cheese
Generous sprinkling of freshly ground black pepper
Pinch of sea salt (optional)

1. Mix all the pastry ingredients except for about a quarter of the egg. Knead on floured worktop for about 5 minutes. Cover with polythene or upturned mixing bowl while you make the filling.
2. Heat the oil, add the water and the *Vecon*. Stir to mix, then add the carrot and cook covered over low heat for 8 minutes. Add leeks and continue gentle cooking for further 8 minutes.
3. Stir in the rolled oats, cook 1 more minute, remove pan from heat.
4. Stir in cottage cheese, and season to taste.
5. Warm and grease a large baking sheet. Set oven to 400°F/200°C (Gas Mark 6).
6. Roll out half the dough at a time without re-kneading to about ⅕-inch (3.5mm) thick. Cut circles using saucer as guide.
7. Place each round on baking sheet, spoon filling along centre then pull sides together to make a pasty shape. Seal and decorate by pressing.
8. Brush with reserved egg and bake for 20-25 minutes.

Opposite: Cheese Chops (page 102) *and* Stuffed Courgettes (page 103).

Savoury Tea Loaf

Why should all tea bread be sweet? This one makes a good snack, plain or toasted, and a handy lunchbox item.

Imperial (Metric)

12 oz (350g) plain wholemeal flour
2 teaspoons baking powder
Large pinch sea salt
¼ teaspoon freshly ground black pepper
1½ oz (40g) soft margarine
3 tablespoons crunchy natural peanut butter
3 sticks celery, finely chopped
3-4 spring onions, finely chopped using green and white parts
3 eggs
¼ pint (140ml) skim milk

1. Set oven to 375°F/190°C (Gas Mark 5).
2. Sift first five ingredients together, rub in margarine.
3. Stir in the peanut butter, celery and onions.
4. Beat the eggs and milk together, add to mixture to make soft dough (add a little extra milk if necessary).
5. Transfer mixture to a large greased loaf tin, bake for 1 hour.

Opposite: American-style Bran Muffins (page 109); Rough Bread (page 108); Oat Bran Biscuits (page 107).

Glossary

Breadcrumbs

Throughout the book, breadcrumbs means fresh, soft wholemeal breadcrumbs, not dried ones, unless specified.

Carob

The bean-like pods of the carob tree have been used since ancient times as a food for animals and humans. The tree grows freely round the Mediterranean and similar climates, the pods dangling have a resemblance to brown broad beans.

The pods used to be sold in sweet shops under the name 'locust beans'. Now they are powdered into a sweet brown 'flour' often used as a substitute for chocolate. The taste isn't very similar, but there's certainly a resemblance.

The advantages of carob are, first, that it is free from the theophylline and caffeine content of chocolate (stimulants). Second, it doesn't contain the substance in chocolate which can set off migraine in some sufferers. Third, it is much lower in fat than cocoa. When made into bars, fat is added; but carob powder is much lower in fat than cocoa. Fourth, chocolate contains oxalic acid, which can combine with calcium to form a compound from which the body cannot extract the calcium. Carob is free from this problem.

Carob powder or flour is obtainable from health food stores. It is added to food in about the same amounts as you would cocoa, sifting into flour in recipes. Carob bars can be gently melted with a knob of butter or margarine to top cakes.

Dropping consistency

Lift a spoonful of the mixture above the bowl and turn sideways. The mixture should slowly drop off.

Eggs

Throughout the book, size 3 eggs are used, unless a small (size 4) or large (size 2) egg is specified.
Free range eggs should be checked carefully before you buy:
● genuinely free range ? Many are not. Ask FREGG (Free Range Egg Association), 37 Tanza Road, London NW3, telephone 01-435 2596. Or follow up producers.

- fresh ? Buy from shops with rapid turnover.
- what do the hens eat ? Prefer producers who make up their own hen food avoiding the yolk colourants standard in commercial blends and medicines often included.

Glazes and fillings

A choice of finishes for bread and cakes:

Egg glaze: Beat egg with a little milk, brush on before baking to give a golden glossy finish.

Honey and nut topping: 10-15 minutes before finishing baking, brush item with honey, which acts as 'glue' for chopped nuts or nut halves, and gives a glossy top.

Honey glaze: Warm a few spoonfuls of honey to soften, adding a very little water. Brush over just after baking to give a soft, sweet finish.

Arrowroot glaze: Mix 2½ fl oz (75ml) fruit juice with scant 1 teaspoon arrowroot. When smooth, bring to the boil, stirring and simmer until mixture clears — a minute or two. Cool, then brush over after baking. If liked, nuts, seeds or dried fruit can be arranged on top of glaze which acts as glue.

Fruit topping: Arrange on top of a cake your choice of nuts, dried apricots or peaches, etc. Boil together equal amounts of honey, water and apricot jam. Drizzle over the topping and leave to make a toffee-like finish.

American white frosting: Traditionally used for carrot cakes, whip 8 oz (225g) low- or medium-fat soft cheese with 1-2 tablespoons honey, to taste, plus a flavouring such as a few drops of natural vanilla; crushed drained pineapple (unsweetened variety); mashed banana and lemon or orange juice (to avoid discolouration); 1-2 teaspoons sieved carob powder or decaffeinated instant coffee; mashed stewed apricots; finely chopped walnuts, etc.

This will make a generous topping for a 7-8-inch (18-20cm) cake. To fill a gateau, you'll need 12-16 oz (350-450g) smooth cheese, depending on the number of layers.

Crème Fraîche

Imperial (Metric)

¼ pint (140ml) double cream
¼ pint (140ml) sour cream or *plain low-fat yogurt*

1. Warm together in a saucepan until just hotter than your finger.
2. Place in a warmed, wide-mouthed vacuum flask, or if not available, in a clean, dry, warmed glass jar. Seal flask or jar. If using jar, place in a airing cupboard.
3. Leave overnight when cream will have thickened. Refrigerate.
4. You can also beat double or sour cream with equal quantities of Quark.

Crème Pâtissière

Imperial (Metric)

½ pint (285ml) skim milk
2 tablespoons honey
1 tablespoon skim milk powder
2 level tablespoons cornflour
1 egg
1 egg yolk
A few drops vanilla essence
1 small knob butter

1. Heat the milk, and beat a little into the mixed honey, skim milk powder, cornflour, egg and egg yolk. When smooth and creamy, add remaining milk.
2. Heat very gently, stirring constantly, until it thickens. Cook for 1 minute.
3. Flavour with vanilla and stir in butter. Cool covered with a disc of wet greaseproof paper to prevent skin forming.
4. You can also mix this half-and-half with whipped cream.

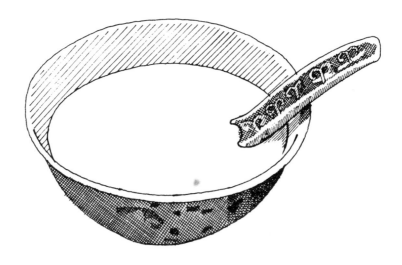

Jam

For best results, use best quality jam. This means either bought or home-made jam free from colourings and preservatives, or the all-fruit, no-added-sugars jams sold under the *Whole Earth* label at health food stores.

Margarine

The phrase 'high pufa' margarine used throughout this book is intended to remind you that all margarines are not equal. While all margarines made from vegetables fats are virtually free from cholesterol, ones which have had most of their oils hardened (or which are made from naturally hard vegetable fats such as palm oil) have little health advantage over hard animal fats. In addition, many margarines do contain animal fats. If you want to benefit from the margarine you buy, choose the kind that is not only soft, but also states on the label that it is high in polyunsaturates. Almost all these will still contain some hardened (hydrogenated) fats (how else can you make oils solid?) but still retain a high proportion of polyunsaturated fatty acids, i.e., are 'high pufa'. These provide the essential fatty acids needed for health. An unusual margarine is *Vitaquell*, where naturally hard vegetable fats are combined with high pufa oils to avoid artificial hardening. This margarine has other advantages: it contains no added salt, no milk products (most soft margarines are unsuitable for milk-free diets), and has a high level of vitamin E. It is sold at health food stores.

If you want to keep some butter in your cooking, why not? Although most people in the West would benefit from eating less fat and in particular, less hard fat, there is no reason why you should not eat and cook with butter and stay well — provided you don't eat the average high amount of animal fats elsewhere in your meals. If you rarely eat cream, red meat, pastry, chocolate, cream cheese, and other high-fat foods, and keep your total intake of animal *and* vegetable fat down to about 3 oz (85g) total per day, a little butter here and there won't hurt you.

Milk

The skim milk used throughout this book has roughly 200-240 calories per pint, depending on whether it is sold with skim milk powder added. This contrasts with some 380 calories per pint for whole milk. The difference is all accounted for by fat. Skim milk has plenty of protein and vitamins, and can be used safely for children provided they eat a varied diet which includes some sources of vitamin A and D. The former is generously provided by leafy green, orange and red fruit or vegetables; the latter by sunlight on the skin; and both by oily fish such as herrings.

Semi-skimmed milk has about 300 calories per pint. If you spoon off the creamy layer at the top of a bottle of non-homogenised milk, you have something very similar to semi-skimmed.

If you want to give more 'body' to milk, stir in 1-2 tablespoons per pint of skim milk powder.

Skim milk can be used in any recipe. It must only be heated slowly, stirring often, as it tends to stick and burn.

Oven temperature

Ovens vary enormously, from Agas which provide the option of a substantially higher top temperature than most domestic ovens, through ovens whose owners know that top, middle and bottom shelves offer quite different heats, to fan ovens, where heat is constant throughout the oven, and food cooks at lower temperatures. Throughout this book, 'middle shelf' is assumed. Most yeast recipes are started off at the oven's top temperature. This is because the opening of the oven door to put bread in will knock down the temperature, especially if several loaves are put in, so reducing the heat inside the oven. The first minutes of baking should provide a final 'kick' to the yeast, producing a last burst of rising. After 10 minutes, the temperatures can be reduced so the inside of the item gets baked through without the outside getting overdone.

It's a good idea when making any new recipe to check progress periodically to see how your oven is behaving compared to the suggested cooking time. If your oven cooks faster or slower, write the time into the recipe for next time.

Fan oven users will need to 'translate' the temperatures given into the equivalents for their particular equipment. Fan ovens generally need a much shorter pre-heating period. (See temperature chart inside the back cover.

Proving

Letting a yeast mixture sit in a warm place to rise is called proving. The yeast feeds off the dough, and produces gas. The gas is caught in the strands of the dough or batter, and these stretch under the pressure, causing the mixture to rise.

Traditional yeast recipes often (not always) call for two provings. This isn't necessary especially if you add vitamin C which speeds the development of the dough. However, long proving or fermentation does make the end result different, and many people prefer it. The long proving has two main results.

1. You need less yeast. Generally speaking, the less yeast used per kilo/pound of flour, the longer the end product will stay fresh.
2. You get a tangier flavour. Visitors to Northern Europe enjoy the huge variety of breads there, and often try to imitate their special, almost sour, flavour when they come home. The secret is long fermentation, often overnight in a cold place. You'll find this method used in the rye bread and sourdough recipes in this book. You can apply it to any bread recipe: omit the vitamin C, mix the dough as usual and place in unwarmed bread tins. Leave covered in a cool place or even the refrigerator for several hours. One way is to mix the dough just before going to bed, and let it rise in polythene-covered tins in the refrigerator overnight. Turn the oven on first thing in the morning and bake.

If bread proves too long, it over-stretches itself. When the heat of the oven stimulates a final spurt of rising, it may well collapse. Don't be tempted to let dough more than double its bulk. If dough does rise too much, don't worry. Simply remove from the tin, re-knead for a minute or two, re-shape and place in tins again. Cover loosely, and the dough will rise again surprisingly quickly in a warm place.

Don't be tempted to try and hurry rising up by placing dough in a low temperature oven or hot airing cupboard (although a cool one is fine). It is too easy to kill the yeast by overheating it. Providing a place that is too cold, on the other hand, will only enormously slow down rising. In most houses, leaving bread tins near but not on the stove is quite satisfactory for rising; avoid draughts.

Rubbing in

A method of mixing fat into flour used in making shortcrust pastry and some biscuits. The fat is cut into small pieces, then using the fingertips of both hands, rubbed in until the mixture looks like breadcrumbs. Avoid letting the mixture get hot by handling it too much.

Rubbing in is often unnecessary when cooking with high pufa margarine, which is soft by nature so can be mixed in with a fork followed by a little hand rubbing in only if the mixture is lumpy.

Sea salt

The National Advisory Committee on Nutrition Education has recommended that we all eat less salt. This is mainly because a high salt intake is associated with high blood-pressure in vulnerable people. High blood-pressure is a symptom of a much higher risk of heart attack or stroke. High salt intake is far from the only factor in high blood-pressure: overweight, smoking, lack of exercise and stress are also important factors we can do something about. Heredity also has a strong influence. Nor does everyone who eats a lot of salt get high blood-pressure. However, some 2 in 5 of the Western population may benefit in blood-pressure terms from eating less salt.

There may be a more general health benefit too, in terms of relieving the body of the effort of getting rid of the large amount of excess salt eaten.

This book minimizes the salt used. You may find the recipes lacking in saltiness if you have a strong taste for salt. If so, it may be worth persevering in order to re-train your taste buds to want less salt. This does happen after several weeks, although most people continue to want some salt in food. Lemon juice, plain yogurt, garlic, onions, herbs and spices are useful flavourings which help food taste good without adding much salt.

The National Advisory Committee suggested that most people would benefit by cutting salt intake from the current average of 12 grams per day to between 5 and 8 grams per day, i.e., roughly half.

This book uses sea salt, not because it contains less salt, but because it provides traces of other minerals which may be useful, particularly iodine. Grinding sea salt in a mill may also make people more aware of how much salt they are adding to food, versus the effortless pouring of regular salt from a salt cellar.

Sugar

Because so little crystal sugar is used in this book, it doesn't matter very much whether you use white or brown. The nutritional differences between them are small.

If you choose brown because you want a more natural food, pick one of the sugars which comes from sugar-growing areas, not a brown sugar made up with beet sugar and molasses. Your choice is, from lightest to most treacly, Demerara, Light Muscovado, Dark Muscovado, Barbados or Molasses sugar. You should see the country of origin as somewhere like Guyana, or Demerara itself, written on the packet, or the term 'raw cane' will be used.

Fructose, also known as fruit sugar or laevulose, is a very white sugar obtained from fruit and trees. It costs much more than white or brown sugar, but tastes substantially sweeter to most people. It can also be digested by most people without producing insulin for the purpose. Many diabetics are allowed to use limited amounts of fructose, but should not do so without getting the agreement of their dietition. In this book, fructose can be used instead of crystal sugar in any recipe, using a little less. If you want to cook generally with larger amounts of fructose, e.g., make jam, you will need special recipes as it behaves differently in some ways. You can obtain these by writing to the manufacturer named on the fructose packet.

Vecon

Vecon is a vegetable concentrate, which comes in a jar. It is a useful way of making a tasty stock, or of giving flavour to foods more subtly than yeast extract does. However, its taste is still very strong, so use in tiny amounts. It is all-natural, so preferable to supermarket stock cubes, which usually feature monosodium glutamate.

Vitamin C

Making dough more acid helps develop the stretchy qualities of the gluten protein. This elasticity is the basis of bread rising. When yeast gives off gas, the elastic strands stretch up under the pressure, forming bubbles. The elasticity develops partly with kneading, and partly through 'proving' — leaving the dough to sit.

Adding vitamin C — ascorbic acid — to dough is an acceptable way of making dough more acid and speeding the development process. The result is that bread can be kneaded once and left to rise once only, instead of the traditional twice, without spoiling the result.

A small amount of vitamin C, about 25-50 milligrams, will suffice for a full 1½ kilo bag of flour. The vitamin C can be added by crushing a vitamin C tablet and adding to the liquid in the recipe; but the easiest way is to buy a small tub of vitamin C powder, and add very small amounts direct to the flour.

Little of the vitamin C will survive the heat of cooking, so this addition does not markedly help your vitamin intake.

Yeast

The newer type of small particle or 'micronized' yeast is used throughout this book, because it speeds recipes by making it unnecessary to mix yeast with liquid before adding to the main mixture. This yeast is often sold in wholefood stores in larger, more economical sizes than the more common sachets, under the name 'Fermipan'. However, if you prefer to use either fresh compressed yeast or larger particle dried yeast, do so.

If using fresh yeast, allow 1 oz (25g) to each 1½ lb (680g) flour in the recipe. Mash in a cup with some of the warm (110°F=43°C) liquid from the recipe, and a teaspoonful of honey, sugar or flour. You do not have to measure the temperature of the liquid exactly: it should be a little hotter than your finger, but only comfortably warm.

If using large particle dried yeast, allow ½ oz (15g) to each 1½ lb (680g) flour in the recipe. Whisk with a fork into a cupful of the warm liquid from the recipe and leave to stand for about 10 minutes, until you have a frothy 'head' on the yeast, as on a pint of stout. The temperature should be the same as for fresh yeast, above.

Using liquid that is too cool will delay yeast reaction, but not kill the organism. But using hot water will kill yeast. A good rule of thumb is to divide the liquid in a recipe by three. By boiling one third of the amount, then mixing with remaining two-thirds cold, you will achieve the correct temperature.

Fresh yeast is sold by the ounce from the chilled cabinet in health food stores. Some bakers will also sell it to you . Keep it wrapped in the refrigerator for not more than 10 days.

Index

Edited by Miriam Polunin

FAST FOOD — REAL FOOD

Healthy and Enjoyable Meals — On the Table Within 10 to 30 Minutes

A new and expanded edition of this popular book which proves that fast food need not be junk food, and that all the family can eat healthily without anyone having to spend hours over a hot stove — and without having to resort to microwave or freezer, packets or cans.

Here is a wealth of information and advice for the busy cook, including time-saving tips, advice on menu planning, and general nutritional guidelines. All the recipes use wholesome, natural foods, are high in fibre, low in salt and sugar, and avoid saturated fats. Cooking techniques are designed to avoid the loss of precious minerals and vitamins, retaining all the goodness of the food whilst bringing its appetizing natural flavour to the fore.

Illustrated including 8 colour plates.